ASTROLOGY AND HOROSCOPE ARE A TYPE OF PSEUDOSCIENCE

Austin

Koeckeritz

ABSTRACT

A Pseudoscience consists of statements, beliefs, or practices that are claimed to be both scientific and factual, but are incompatible with the scientific method. Statistics show that the recent upsurge in interests for horoscopes and astrological predictions may not be disconnected from the belief that astrology is in some way scientific, and that it is able to offer explanatory insights and foresights (predictions) into many of life's complexities. This study scrutinizes the "scientificness" of astrology and finds that it falls short of the scientific method, is flawed by its inherent theoretical inconsistencies and has been invalidated by several empirical tests. Astrology gains its relevance today from the vulnerabilities imposed by the stress of burgeoning social complexities, and it sustains participatory interest through the fragile sense of succor that it gives through the Barnum Effect and Subjective Validation. The study evaluates the mystical and mythological origins of astrology as a culturally transmitted heuristics, the stagnancy of its explanatory power for about four millennia despite advances in human knowledge (such as the discovery of the precession of the equinoxes which automatically alters its zodiacal order and reduces astrological charts to mere abstractions), its posture of inerrancy and confirmation bias for scanty supportive tests in spite of the numerous empirical invalidations of its theories, and its lack of openness to systematic practices and the scientific method in developing sound theories. The study observes that astrology is inflicted with all the trappings of a failed science, its predictions have no empirical credibility, but are merely generalized conjectures designed to fit all situations. The study concludes that astrology is a pseudoscience and that its theories have no empirical authenticity.

TABLE OF CONTENTS

LIST OF TABLES AND DIAGRAMS

Tables

Diagrams

Introduction

Michael Shermer, one of the leading scientists to have gone all out to verify the scientific character of astrology and other pseudoscience forms has defined the term pseudoscience as "claims presented so that they appear [to be] scientific even though they lack supporting evidence and plausibility"[1]. In contrast, science has been defined as the intellectual and practical activity encompassing the systematic study of the structure and behavior of the physical and natural world through observation and experiment. Scientists generally agree that the earliest roots of science as we know it today can be traced to Ancient Egypt and Mesopotamia in around 3500 to 3000 BCE where important contributions were made to mathematics, astronomy, and medicine. Astronomy as it is known today originated in astrology which was the predominant undertaking during the earliest periods of the search into the knowledge of the celestial bodies and their relevance to terrestrial life. These contributions later shaped Greek natural philosophy of classical antiquity, with organized measures taken to study the natural causes of existing phenomena in the physical world.

[1]Michael Shermer (1997). *"Why people believe weird things: pseudoscience, superstition and other confusions of our time"* New York: W. H. Freeman and Company. ISBN0-7167-3090-1.

Astrology consists of a number of notions and belief systems that hold that there is a causal relationship between celestial bodies and the course of human events or the description of individual personalities and their roots in the human world. It is a search for human meaning in the possible connotations of celestial alignments in the sky, derived from traditions of early civilizations and their beliefs in the influence of deities in human affairs especially in relation to such events as seasonal changes, plagues, war, political tensions and complex social changes. This text takes a good look at the characteristics of Astrology and juxtaposes these characteristics with established principles of science in order to probe the validity of the scientific appearance that astrologers impute to their craft and are wont to defend albeit with little or no substantial proof. The nature, origin, forms, methods and characteristic manifestations of astrology are contextually construed within the relevance of their validity to scientific knowledge, and by extension their usefulness within the same scientific context to the betterment of human life.

CHAPTER ONE
IS ASTROLOGY A SCIENCE?

There seems to be a growing consciousness and a new wave of attention for the suppositions of Astrology, with many people not knowing exactly how to distinguish between what is scientific on the one hand, from claims that are unscientific on the other hand. According to the United States National Science Foundation (NSF) in a 2014 report, Americans showed they are more likely to have a "great deal of confidence" in leaders of the scientific community, yet the unanimous rejection of the notion of astrology as a science[2] by the organized science

[2]*Zarka, Philippe "Astronomy and Astrology". Proceedings of the International Astronomical Union. 5 (S260): 420–*

community doesn't seem to make a strong enough imprint on the minds of people, especially considering the recent surge in the positive perceptions given to astrological interpretations. A recent survey published by the NSF in the same 2014 report[3]states that in 2012, slightly more than half of Americans said astrology was "not at all scientific," whereas nearly two-thirds gave this same response in 2010. Looking back at the reports about a decade ago, nine percent of those questioned in the NSF survey of 2001[4], said that astrology was "very scientific" and 32 percent answered "sort of scientific" (thus a combined sum of 41% of respondents favored some scientific

425 (2011)..

[3] National Science Foundation, "*Science and Engineering Indicators 2014*" National Center for Science and Engineering Statistics (NCSES), Arlington, VA (NSB 14-01), February 2014. Retrieved from: https://www.nsf.gov/statistics/seind14/index.cfm/chapter-7/c7h.htm

[4]National Science Foundation, "*Science and Engineering Indicators 2001*" National Center for Science and Engineering Statistics (NCSES), Arlington. Retrieved from: https://wayback.archive-it.org/5902/20150818104004/http://www.nsf.gov/statistics/seind02/c7/c7s5.htm

coloration to astrology, 4 percent said they don't know and 56 percent gave an outright negative to the scientific claims of astrology). Reports by online media groups suggest that there has been a great surge in the attention given to horoscope predictions going by the number of visits to horoscope sections on online media platforms. *Gallup* reports show a survey analysis that 25 percent of the American and Canadian society in 2005 believed in horoscopes, while it is at 24 percent for Britons. Stella Bugbee, editor-in-chief of an online medium *The Cut*, says a typical horoscope post on the site got 150 percent more traffic in 2017 than in 2016[5]. All these are pointers to the burgeoning cultural trends that have begun to situate horoscopic lingo in today's ever-evolving social parlance.

The critical question however borders on identifying what makes a field or body of knowledge scientific. Should high sounding terminologies in astrology such as constellations, ecliptic longitude,

---

[5] Julie Beck (2018), "The New Age of Astrology", published in *The Atlantic*, June 16 2018.

natal chart, zodiac quadrants, cardinal, fixed & mutable modes, axis pairs, ephemeris—and other terminologies it shares with the pure scientific field of astronomy—be used as a subconscious inference of its scientific qualities or credibility? It is therefore important to verify the basis for the scientific claims of astrology and determine the quality of its ranking, if any, against other established fields of science and in the light of the standard measures used in the scientific process.

1.1 ASTROLOGY AND THE SCIENTIFIC METHOD

Science according to Shermer (1997, p. 17) is *"a set of methods designed to describe and interpret observed and inferred phenomena, past or present, and aimed at building a testable body of knowledge open to rejection or confirmation"*[6]. The quest to

[6]Michael Shermer (1997). *"Why people believe weird things: pseudoscience, superstition and other confusions of our time"* New York: W. H. Freeman and Company. ISBN0-7167-3090-1.

always clearly demarcate an organized body of scientific knowledge from myths, popular wit and wisdom or from mystical analogies, has been an on-going concern among established thinkers and those who have propounded scientific theories for many years. For instance, Aristotle had asserted that science must use logical demonstration and must identify the universals which exist as a nature in the particulars of sense with incontrovertible certainty. According to the Oxford English Dictionary 2019, science is *"The intellectual and practical activity encompassing the systematic study of the structure and behaviour of the physical and natural world through observation and experiment"*. An important ingredient which this definition adds is the centrality of observation and experiment in the process of determining the scientific nature of any interpretation of natural phenomena. Therefore, for Astrology to put on the garb of science properly, it has to present unambiguous, provable and non-conflicting claims. When claims are ambiguous, they are open to more than one interpretation and have no definite meaning or outcome in relation to particular phenomena. But this has often characterized many population studies carried out to test astrological claims.

Often it has been discovered that the zodiac traits attributable to specified groups are though clearly stated, but do not produce determinate outcomes and many times apply in conflicting ways to a wider cross-section of people grouped under them. This makes the claims conflict with the observable outcomes with large inconsistencies, which by default cast a shadow on their scientific credibility. Astrology's chief claim is that there are correspondences between <u>celestial observations</u> (of the stars, planets, the moon and the sun) and <u>terrestrial events</u>, and it seeks to interpret and predict information about human affairs by studying the movements and relative positions of these celestial objects, ascribing laid down inferences to the readings from its charts. In essence, according to astrology events on earth, such as in a country or in people's lives are shaped and influenced by the positioning and alignments of these celestial objects from time to time. It uses four major predictive methods—i.e. the Solar and Lunar returns, progressions, horary astrology, and transits—which will be discussed later in this book. A systematic way of proving or disproving a theory is at the heart of science and is the basis for ascribing the scientific reputation to any field of study. Until the 17th century, astrology was considered a scientific field, and it essentially kicked-off any knowledge drive in the <u>development of astronomy</u>—astronomy has since distinguished itself through the scientific process as a scientific enterprise. Astrology on the other hand was commonly accepted in early political and cultural circles as scientific, with some of its concepts regularly used in classical discourses, traditional studies, and climate/seasonal interpretations in influential civilizations of the various Islamic, Roman, Babylonian, Egyptian and other strategic eras across various cultures. However, by the 17th century, it lost its academic appeal when scholarly explanations of the role of celestial bodies emerged in Astronomy as a more thorough endeavor from the generalizations of Astrology, thus leading to the successful Siamese separation of the hitherto conjoined fields.

The scientific method is an epistemological system for deriving and developing knowledge through a process that tests its validity, justification and rationality. The prime focus of the modern scientific method is that observations are made and later developed into scientific guesses (i.e. hypotheses) and theories. These observations must culminate in:

➢ **Falsifiable predictions**, that can be tested against
➢ **Empirical reality**, and that are based on the posture of
➢ **Naturalism** (i.e. a posture of reliance on natural causes as against supernatural causes).

Essentially, the following six steps make up the scientific method:

1. Observation: This involves taking note of things in the environment with curiosity.

2. Hypothesis: Thinking up a possible explanation after close observation.

3. Prediction: Making falsifiable predictions based on the hypothesis formed; a hypothesis that will be further tested to prove its validity or otherwise.

4. Test/Experiment Prediction: Compare the predictions with new empirical evidence from experiments which could disprove the original hypothesis and lead to the formulation of a more refined one.

5. Reproducibility/Repeatability: This refers to the possibility of reproducing same result of an experiment if carried out by a third party who follows the same procedures.

6. The Double-Blind Principle: This describes any decision process where all parties directly involved in a test are not given vital information so as to avoid casting a bias on the outcome. Both the experimenter and the observers in the experiment do not know which of the subjects are in the "experimental

group" and which are in the "control group", so that both are blind to what aspect of the experiment they are conducting.

Unlike astrology, astronomy has subjected its findings on a continual basis to the rigors of the scientific process indicated above, and where necessary it has discarded hitherto existing theories that have been disproven in new tests. But astrology seems to have an inherent fixation to the inerrancy of its foundational principles even in the face of the serious implications of new empirical findings to its theories; a case in point is the discovery of the "precession of the equinoxes", which findings show has overtime changed the earth's position to sun[7]. This posture clearly removes it from being a scientific field, as

---

[7] Ancient astrologers were unaware of the fact that the Earth wobbles continually around its axis in a 25,772-year cycle. This wobble is due to the gravitational attraction of the sun and the moon on the Earth's equatorial bulge and this radically alters the earlier zodiacal positions previously adopted by Astrologers in their constellations but which they have clung to.

science is perpetually refined by the principle of falsifiability. Later on in this text, some of the experiments carried out to prove the claims of astrology will be considered, and the inherent contradictions emerging therefrom will be evaluated against the backdrop of some arguments and disputations from the astrological community.

1.2 THE ORIGINS OF ASTROLOGY

Astrology has been dated by some to at least the 2nd millennium BCE, some others say there are traces as far as the 3rd millennium BC, with its primary roots in calendrical systems used to predict seasonal shifts; while further on it was used in the divining of political outcomes, social changes, and the interpretation of celestial cycles as signs of the involvement of divine entities in human affairs. There is some evidence to suggest that the oldest known astrological references are copies of texts made during this period, particularly in Mesopotamia (Sumer, Akkad, Assyria and Babylonia)[8].

---

[8]E. F. Weidner, 'Historiches Material in der

The first system of organized astrology has been linked to **Babylonian astrology** which is indicated to have arisen in the 2nd millennium BC[9]. Scholarly celestial readings are generally reported to have begun with the oldest Babylonian texts dated at c.1800 BC, and continued through to c.1200 BC, and they capture what historians refer to as the Middle Babylonian/Assyrian periods. Astrology was primarily used to analyze seasonal changes, interpret political undertones and seek appeasement of the gods in the interest of the king or the state.

The Egyptians had what is known as **Decanic Astrology** which involved a reading of the position of 36 groups of stars used in **Ancient Egyptian astronomy**. These groups of stars seemed to rise in a systematic manner on the horizon when the earth completed a rotation. The consistency in the *decan* was then used to mark 'hours' and groups of 10 days

---

BabyonischenOmina-Literatur' *AltorientalischeStudien*, ed. Bruno Meissner, (Leipzig, 1928-9), v. 231 and 236.
[9]Holden, James Herschel (1996), *"A History of Horoscopic Astrology". AFA p. 1. ISBN 978-0-86690-463-6*

which culminated in an Egyptian year, with the cycle repeated after each turn. This started in the 9th or 10th Dynasty (c. 2100 BCE) and was used as a star clock to measure time and seasons[10]. However, Egyptian astrology came under Hellenistic influence when Egypt was occupied by Alexander the Great in 332 BC. The scholars of Alexandria were prolific and their influence grew consistently. In Ptolemaic Alexandria, the Egyptian tradition of Decanic astrology came under the modifications brought in from Babylonian astrology and thus birthed Horoscopic astrology. Horoscopic traditions are steeped in a belief that the placement of the planets at any given moment in time is a reflection of the nature of that moment, and anything born at that time, whether a person or nation or relationship will be influenced by the implications of such a moment.

---

[10]Symons, S.L., Cockcroft, R., Bettencourt, J. and Koykka, C. (2013). "Ancient Egyptian Astronomy" [Online database]. Available at: https://aea.physics.mcmaster.ca/index.php/en/database/dia gonal-star-tables

Hellenistic Astrology as explained by popular historian Nicholas Campion shows how the innovation of Babylonian Astrological findings and theories moved west to the Hellenistic world of Greece, and Greece in turn played a crucial role in the transmission of astrological theory to Rome. The conquest of Asia by Alexander the Great exposed the Greeks to Syrian, Babylonian and Persian cosmology; though Greek as a language became the language of intellectual communication across the region, however the cosmological ideas were essentially not Greek in origin, but were translated to Greek and then transmitted through Greek as the language of intellectual communication[11]. Early signs in Rome of the attribution of astrology to the use of magic were in the 1st century CE, and at this time it was considered treasonable. Under Emperor Nero, one Publius Anteius was accused of the crime of funding an outlawed astrologer Pammenes, and was forced to

[11]Campion, Nicholas (2008), *"A History of Western Astrology, Vol. 1: The Ancient World", (first published as The Dawn of Astrology: a Cultural History of Western Astrology). London Continuum. ISBN 9781441181299.*

commit suicide as punishment for this crime[12]. There are evidences that the astral omens employed in Mesopotamian divination were later commingled with what remained jointly known in this period as astrology; this formed within astrology a branch described as natural astrology[13].

During the **Islamic Golden Age,** astrology was taken up enthusiastically by Islamic scholars following the collapse of Alexandria to the Arabs in the 7th century, which led to the founding of the Abbasid Empire in the 8th century. Caliph Al Mansur (754-775), the second Abbasid Caliph, built Baghdad as the central city of learning which housed the *Bayt al-Hikma* translated as the 'Storehouse of Wisdom' for Arabic translations of Hellenistic theories and knowledge, including astrological texts[14]. These texts

---

[12]Rudich, Vasily (2005). *"Political Dissidence Under Nero: The Price of Dissimulation". Routledge. Pp. 145–146. ISBN 9781134914517.*

[13] Robert Andrew Gilbert and David E. Pingree. "Astrology". Encyclopaedia Britannica.

[14]Houlding Deborah (2010), *"Essays on the history of western astrology",* 'The Medieval Development of Hellenistic Principles Concerning Aspectual Applications

were directly influential upon subsequent European astrologers such as Guido Bonatti in the 13th century, and William Lilly in the 17th century. Knowledge of Arabic texts started to be imported into Europe during the Latin translations of the 12th century and the Arabs made far reaching contributions to the knowledge of cosmology and astrological concepts in Europe. As the theoretical knowledge of Islam began to gain new grounds, some of the practices of astrology were hotly contended against on theological grounds. These criticisms centered on the fact that the methods of astrologers were conjectural rather than empirical, and conflicted with the proper religious contexts of Islamic teachings especially in relation to horary astrology that linked the reading of stars to predicting the fates of people[15].

The earliest work of **Hindu Astrology** to have survived is the *Vedanga Jyotisha*, and it contains the

---

and Orbs'; *Nottingham: STA* Ch. 8, pp.12-13.
[15]Saliba, George, (1994). *"A History of Arabic astronomy: planetary theories during the Golden Age of Islam"*. New York University Press. Pp.60-69. *ISBN 0-8147-7962-X.*

techniques employed in interpreting the movements of the sun and the moon based on a five-year calendar cycle. The dating of this work is uncertain, and is suggested to be as far back as 2nd millennium BC, with certain other evidences pointing to its prominence in a few centuries BC[16]. The more recent sense of modern horoscopic astrology in India is however linked to the meeting of the Indian and Hellenistic cultures during the Indo-Greek period[17]at which time Greek became a lingua franca of the Indus valley region due to the military conquest of Bactria by Alexander the Great. Indian astronomy and astrology developed together with the earliest treatises dating from the Vedic era, which were written on specially prepared tree barks. The Samhita Compilation is amazingly said to contain five million horoscopes divining both past and future events of

---

[16]*Sastry, T.S.K, K.V. Sarma, (ed.) (1985)."Vedangajyotisa of Lagadha"*. National Commission for the Compilation of History of Sciences in India by Indian National Science Academy.
[17]Pingree, David, (1981) *"Jyotiḥśāstra, Wiesbaden: Otto Harrassowitz" (1981)* p.81.

those who have lived (in the past, and the major highlights to their lives) and those who will live (in the future and the major events that will mark their lives and time).

Chinese Astrology which came into prominence under the Han Dynasty (2nd century BC to 2nd century AD) has interesting measures of distinctiveness from the general flow of the astrological cultures earlier mentioned. It is largely based on astronomy and calendars[18]with a close relation with the Chinese theory of the three fold harmony—i.e. of heaven, earth and water; and it uses special astrological principles that are not found in other regions such as the principles of yin and yang, the Wu Xing teachings, the 10 Celestial stems, the 12 Earthly Branches, the lunisolar calendar (i.e. moon calendar and sun calendar), *Shichen*, and the year, month and day time calculations. It has some form of ~~affiliation with general west~~ern astrology through the

[18]*Pankenier, David W., (2013). "Astrology and Cosmology in Early China: Conforming Earth to Heaven", Cambridge University Press ISBN 9781107292246.*

twelve animal signs of the zodiac as documented since the Shang (Shing or Yin) dynasty (ca 1766 BC – ca 1050 BC) and the 60-year cycle combining five elements with these twelve zodiac signs.

Maya and **Aztec** **Astrology** of Pre-Columbian Mesoamerica had a common system in use throughout the region, dating back to at least the 6th century BC. The earliest calendars were employed by peoples such as the Zapotecs, Olmecs, Maya, Mixtec and Aztecs. The Mesoamerican astrological calendar definitely did not originate with the Maya, though they made a lot of subsequent expansions and improvements and rose to be the most sophisticated in its use. Along with those of the Aztecs, the Maya calendars are attested to be the best-documented and most completely understood. The Mayan calendar used the solar year of 360 days, which governed the planting of crops and other domestic matters; and the Tzolkin of 260 days; and both had an elaborate astrological system to cover every facet of life. A 584-day Venus cycle was also in place and had a strong influence on the Mayan culture so that Mayan rulers often planned the beginning of warfare to coincide with when Venus rose and in many cases did the same in other areas with Mercury, Mars and Jupiter, and possessed a zodiac of some kind. The Aztec calendar had the same basic structure as the Mayan calendar, with two main cycles of 360 days and 260 days; these two cycles formed a 52-year "century" called the calendar round.

Astrology in Medieval and Renaissance Europe was affected first by the break-up of the Roman Empire which cut-off the Greek scholarly traditions; then it was checked by the church, which condemned any set of practices that were suspicious or suggestive of diabolic roots or affiliations. It was also influenced by the flourishing fusion and review of Indian, Persian and Islamic cosmology on-going at the time[19].By the 10th century when Arabic works began to be translated into Latin and started making

---

[19] Nick Kanas, (2007). "*Star Maps: History, Artistry, and Cartography*", Springer p.79.

their way to Europe through Spain, astrology began to thrive until it gained good grounds by the 12th century[20]. It is believed that by the 13th century, astrology had become so prominent that it was a part of everyday medical practice in Europe, so that evidences in the 16th century showed medical practitioners were required by law to calculate the position of the Moon in relation to relevant charts before carrying out certain forms of complicated medical procedures[21]. At this time in Europe, in baccalaureate programs, planets were used to represent the seven distinct areas designated as the Liberal arts. Grammar was assigned to the Moon, Dialectics was assigned to Mercury, Rhetoric to Venus, Music to the Sun, Arithmetic to Mars, Geometry to Jupiter and

---

[20] Ibid.

[21] British Library, *"Learning Bodies of Knowledge: Medieval Astrology"*. Available at https://web.archive.org/web/20130305064820/http://www.bl.uk/learning/artimages/bodies/astrology/astrologyhome.html

Astrology/Astronomy to Saturn. British monk Johannes de Sacrobosco, Italian astrologer Guido Bonatti, English astrologer Richard Trewythian, and Astrologer/Astronomer Richard of Wallingford, were among the very prominent astrologers whose works were widely celebrated during this period. Literary giants such as Dante Alighieri and Geoffrey Chaucer made several references in their works to astrological symbols. By the Renaissance when astrology suffered some diminishing criticism, the leading figures in the reappraisal of the standing of its scholarship were themselves initially astrologers and they included prominent men such as Tycho Brahe, Galileo Galilei, Johannes Kepler among others. By the end of the Renaissance, Aristotelian physics had largely been replaced by more accurate theories and so was geocentrism, and the traditional theories on the sublunar and celestial realms. The 16th and 17th century saw new shifts which culminated by the 18th century in a drastic abandonment of the astrological enterprise by the intellectual community for more scientifically coherent methods and provable theories. This made Astrology gravitate towards an isolated and unique divinatory art steeped in ancient mystic methods, traditions and symbolisms.

1.3 ASTROLOGY AND ITS RELEVANCE TO HUMAN LIFE

From the *NSF* and *Gallup* data cited earlier above, there is obviously a growing trend of reliance on horoscopes today that has given astrology a whole new face in social relations. It is not uncommon to find young, energetic and promising young people checking out what their zodiac signs say, while a growing number of full grown adults[22]know their signs. There are also a retinue of special websites feeding senior citizens with horoscopes specially curated for them. Since the rise of the New Age movement, Astrology had maintained a regular

---

[22] Nicholas Campion (2017). "How Many People Actually Believe in Astrology". *The Conversation* (April 26, 2017), Boston. Available at http://theconversation.com/how-many-people-actually-believe-in-astrology-71192

appearance, albeit on the back pages of prominent newspapers and magazines, but the recent boom is being facilitated by the internet revolution, especially because of the barriers to access that it surmounts quite easily.

Despite the successful disputations on the credibility of astrology as a science, its inherent methods and body of knowledge seem to create a fascinating appeal for the realm of the unknown, with the trappings of its special terminologies and the instruments of its craft which give a lot of people an impression of its scientific prospects. The veiled mysteries astrology claims to uncover and the curiosity this posture evokes could be said to be one of the reasons for the attention it is getting. This is because a lot of people want to have an idea of what tomorrow brings today, so that they can prepare their minds and align themselves accordingly. Commentaries from pundits and the results of various interviews point to the fact that the relevance of astrology is not in its ability to accurately interpret the zodiac constellations in relation to human affairs in an empirically and scientifically consistent manner, its relevance is the pacifying and substitutionary explanation it seems to provide for the complex social problems, irregularities, intangibles and the constantly heightened anxiety with which people navigate their daily lives. The proliferation and easy access to horoscopic interpretations as against for instance the scientific but more inaccessible offerings of the organized field of psychology is another good pointer to why people go for the more available astrology, and the timeous predictions it seems to offer in critical areas as relationships, business and career success. Even when these predictions don't have the necessary poofs, people seem more inclined to explain or excuse this away while conditioned by seemingly situational compulsion to steal more peeps into the "likely futures" of their endeavors and determine whether to proceed or refrain from them in the light of the predicted outcomes from horoscopes. The major observations made from these trends suggest that a lot of people, especially youths, pander to the services of astrology for the following reasons:

1. **Personal Stress and Societal Uncertainties**: More and more people today suffer from emotional, economic, career and psychological forms of stress among others due to several factors such as the growing rate of failed relationships, daily strenuous demands on individual capacities, family pressures, difficulties in academic and career pursuits, alarming rise in debilitating social statistics, tensions on belief systems and the uncertain political climates. These factors prompt a curiosity to know the future beforehand and at least have some form of explanation of the prevalent circumstances that can guide their decision making. People want to have hope of a better future in the midst of life's turmoil and they seek to make better decisions, but need a guide for such imprecise situations, which science with all its goodies doesn't seem to readily offer.

2. **Understanding of One's self and Insight into the Personality of Others:** People have a desire for self-understanding and to figure out their place in the world. They also want to be able to interpret the personality of others within the same context. These factors could explain the growing attraction to horoscopes outside the concepts of personality types explained in psychology.

3. **Predictions on Relationships:** Romance is an aspect of social life that pervades the discussions and daily experiences of people. Knowing who is suited for them and what time is more probable for relationship success is a major drive for today's consultation of horoscopes.

4. **Influence of Greater Forces:** Social relations among young people today tends to favor the influence of some kind of force or forces that shape human activities beyond human control. Reasons for this growing trend is doubtful despite the fact that a good number of people

have a tendency to shy away from religious discourses or topics of faith.

5. **Bandwagon Effect:** More people are perhaps simply following the cultural trend just to be part of the fun and not necessarily because they are convinced about the effect of horoscopes, however with the increasing interests, it is difficult not to say their fondness of it has over time grown.

1.4 BRANCHES OF ASTROLOGY AND GROWING TRENDS

Western Astrology—which has inherited influences handed down from the earliest links from Babylonia through to the Islamic golden age—is a broad field, but it can be classified into four major branches which in themselves have several sub-divisions. These major divisions are:

1. Mundane Astrology: This is the aspect of astrology used to predict world affairs and events. It branched out from Judicial Astrology.

2. Electional Astrology: This branch of astrology focuses on choosing the right time for a particular event in the light of astrological analysis.

3. Natal Astrology: Here horoscopes are used to determine an individual's personality and their path in life.

4. Horary Astrology: Under this category of astrology, the astrologer seeks to answer specific questions by constructing a horoscope for that particular time so as to answer the questions.

Some of the other subdivisions under these are Medical Astrology, Psychological Astrology, Financial Astrology, Relationship Astrology among many others.

The new interests that have put astrology on a revived and fanciful pedestal are largely internet-based. From the aesthetic use of words, images, ideas, and concepts through memes, social media handles, social pages, group chats, blogs etc., to diverse forms of astrological advocacy, rebranding techniques, skill sophistication and the use of innovative technology such as digital apps among others, it is clear that there is a buzzing online culture that is fueling this new drift. It was Julie Beck, of *The Atlantic,* an online magazine, who said that "the availability of more in-depth information online has given this cultural wave of astrology a certain erudition"[23]. Amanda Hess[24] makes some clearer points about the trend and observes that:

---

[23] *"The New Age of Astrology",* published in The Atlantic, (January 16 2018). Retrieved at:
https://www.theatlantic.com/health/archive/2018/01/the-new-age-of-astrology/550034/
[24] Amanda Hess (2019), *"How Astrology Took Over The Internet"*, retrieved at
https://www.nytimes.com/2018/01/01/arts/how-astrology-took-over-the-internet.html.

- "...the astrology <u>boomlet</u> owes as much to the dynamics of the modern internet as it does to any sort of cosmic significance about the millennial's place in the universe.

- "...these new online products advance the game by offering seemingly endless customizations. <u>Co-Star</u>[25] bills itself as "hyper-personalized astrology," serving "algorithmically-generated insights personalized to a degree unattainable elsewhere." Its name implies that every user has a supporting role in the drama of the universe..."

- "Modern horoscope apps and columns are also fitted to satisfy up-to-the-minute psychological fixations."

- "Other internet-savvy astrologers are explicitly branding their practices as <u>tools of the #resistance</u>, looking to planetary alignments to shed light on the machinations

---

[25] Co-star is a digital astrological app that offers special astrological services to users.

of the tax bill or Russian election meddling" (in the United States).

➤ "A lot of the updated signals are aesthetic ones. Old-school astrological images of constellations and line-drawn star signs have been replaced by pastel illustrations and mixed media collages. The dominant look is nostalgic but not staid."

These important observations made by Hess and the duplicities catering to various age groups, give a good insight into the publicity image that astrology is adopting to attract and sustain the culture of interest by its growing number of enthusiasts. These developments are fast influencing discussions on politics, romantic relationships, business and finance, psychology, health and wellness goals, family life and other areas of daily living.

CHAPTER TWO

HOROSCOPES

A horoscope is a diagram or chart used to capture the positions of the Sun, Moon and planets, in order to predict future events or give applicative interpretations in relation to the signs of the zodiac. In essence, a horoscope is a prediction chart that uses traditional astrological entries in relation to the position of the Sun and relevant celestial bodies to generate applicable information, analyses and predictions for interested followers in respect to each person's zodiac signs.

2.1 THE ZODIAC AND HOROSCOPIC ASTROLOGY

(a) The Zodiac

In Western Astrology, the Zodiac refers to an area of outer space seen from earth in the sky, extending from about 8° North and 8° South of the celestial latitude of the ecliptic, including all apparent positions of the sun, moon, and most familiar planets over the course of a year. It is divided into twelve equal areas (constellations), each occupying 30° of celestial longitude. The names given to the twelve zodiac constellations are Aries, Taurus, Gemini, Cancer, Leo, Virgo, Libra, Scorpio, Sagittarius, Capricorn, Aquarius and Pisces. These are the twelve astrological names (each having a symbol) that take the ecliptic as the origin of latitude and take the sun's position from the vernal equinox as the origin of longitude. It is believed that the Zodiac originated in Babylonian civilization, and that the current Zodiac as we know it was developed by the Greeks[26]. The word

[26] Hand, Robert (1981). *"Horoscope Symbols"*,

"Zodiac" itself originates from the ancient Greek *"zoidiakos kyklos" (meaning circle of animals)* and given in the Latin translation as *"zodiacus"*.

Though the discovery of the "precession of the equinoxes" as has been earlier referred to—i.e. the wobbling motion of the earth on its axis—has cast a theoretical inconsistency on the exactness of the physical constellations occupied by the signs. Much more, the nature of their different positions makes them occupy divergent widths of the Ecliptic, so that Virgo for instance has been observed to occupy five times more of the ecliptic longitude than Scorpio, however in astrological circles they are ascribed with equality in size and by extension equality in the transitory time period of the sun across each of them. The twelve signs are a combination of animals and mythological characters, and they represent the symbols for the different personality make-ups, traits and fates according to astrological traditions. As shown below, each Latinized zodiac sign—their

Whitford Press, Pennsylvania, USA, p. 183.

English names are added—captures a particular period in which people, things or events are born.

Table 1: Zodiac Signs and Time Periods

Latin Name	English Name	Time Period (Tropical Zodiac)
Aries	The Ram	21 March—20 April
Taurus	The Bull	21 April—21 May
Gemini	The Twins	22 May—21 June
Cancer	The Crab	22 June—22 July
Leo	The Lion	23 July—22 August
Virgo	The maiden	23 August—23 September
Libra	The Scales	24 September—23 October
Scorpio	The Scorpion	24 October—22 November
Sagittarius	The Archer	23 November—21 December
Capricorn	The Sea Goat	22 December—20 January
Aquarius	The Water	21 January—19

	Bearer	February
Pisces	The Fish	20 February—20 March

The Tropical Zodiac is the yearly cycle adopted during the Hellenistic period and predominant in Western Astrology. There are also other yearly cycles such as the Sidereal Zodiac year cycle, and the International Astronomy Union year cycle. The Tropical Zodiac year has been adopted within the scope of this study as the astrological year used in Western Astrology.

A thirteenth constellation had long been identified by the Babylonians, however because they had a lunar calendar year, they were more convenient with the twelve divisions and stuck with it as a measure of their yearly cycle. This thirteenth constellation or area also proven by modern astronomy is called *Ophiuchus* which interjects between Scorpio and Sagittarius.

The twelve zodiac constellations are paired along with what astrologers consider to be the four elements, i.e. Fire, Earth, Air, and Water. The pairings below identify zodiac constellations that are believed to be associated with each of the elements in different measures.

1. Fire: Aries, Leo, Sagittarius—hot, dry, ardent.
2. Earth: Taurus, Virgo, Capricorn—heavy, cold, dry.
3. Air: Gemini, Libra, Aquarius—light, hot, wet.
4. Water: Cancer, Scorpio, Pisces—cold, wet, soft.

These pairs are also called *triplicities,* and each constellation in each pair is said to be 120° apart from the other. Thus, in the first instance you have the Aries, which is a fire constellation, but before the next fire constellation (which is Leo), you have Taurus, Gemini and Cancer coming up in between; and then it gets to Leo and passes through Virgo, Aquarius and Scorpio before it reaches Sagittarius to complete its turn. In like manner, the same 120° measure applies to the other elemental pairs.

These combinations of elemental pairs and the traits associated with each of the signs are very relevant in constructing astrological charts today.

(b) Horoscopic Astrology

Horoscopic Astrology is a form of astrology that takes into account a reading of the alignment of the planets at a particular moment in order to deduce the nature and inherent meaning of such a moment, and ascribe certain qualities, orchestrations, predictions and fates to whatever is or was born at such a time; be it a person, relationship, country, business, project etc. It is the interpretation of these planetary alignments that forms the basis for predictions in relation to the course of events. What makes an astrological field to be categorized as horoscopic is the use of the *Ascendant,* which implies the use of the Eastern horizon rising against the backdrop of the *Ecliptic* in determining the reading of the specific moment under consideration. Horoscopes are thus the *ascendant* interpretation of the current alignments of planetary bodies in connection to their relevance to the various signs of the zodiac in other to make predictions or give meaning to earthly events at individual, interpersonal, group and universal levels.

These predictions, the various methods, theories and their interpretations in relation to divining earthly events have severally been proven to be inaccurate[27] and have been called into question as mere abstractions, inconsistent guesses and speculations, made under broad and widely generalized approximations so as to accommodate a wide range of possible outcomes and thus validate the questionable forecasts. As we will expatiate later in this study, modern discoveries about the true nature of celestial objects have created a big gulf between the theories of astrology and the reconciliation of its predictive claims based on the now proven

---

[27] Jeffrey Bennett; Meghan Donohue; Nicholas Schneider; and Mark Voit (2007). *"The Cosmic Perspective"*, 4th Edition. Pearson/Addison-Wesley, Francisco CA, pp82-84.

inaccuracies of its initial celestial theories. More so, the empirically inconsistent outcomes of its predictions lend greater doubts to the credibility of its methods, claims and assertions.

2.2 THE BARNUM EFFECT AND SUBJECT VALIDATION

The following criterion has been suggested as an important way of determining whether a particular claim is a science or pseudoscience. If a new scientific idea is presented, it should be capable of creating interests that scientist could adopt in their research programs. Scientists could also use the new line of thinking to produce other new lines of research. The new theory should have the potential to lead to other discoveries (Shermer Michael, 1997). It should also be able to influence any existing models, hypotheses, or paradigms. Horoscopes and astrology fail when viewed from this criteria. For instance the use of Barnum Effect is one way to see why horoscopic astrology is a type of pseudoscience.

The Barnum Effect (B.E.) is what promotes the pseudoscience behind astrology and horoscopes. It is believed that the expression Barnum Effect first appeared in 1956 in the essay "Wanted – A Good Cookbook" by psychologist Paul Meehl. The term Barnum Effect is also associated with the popular P. T. Barnum's statement that a "sucker" is born every minute, since Barnum had mastered ways of making the gullible part with their money.

In defining B.E., it has been explained as an occurrence in psychology where people receive interpretations about themselves and their situations, giving high ratings to these descriptions because they directly applied to them. Scrutiny of these descriptions however reveals that they are statements of vague generalities that can apply to anyone. However, when perceived to be coming from an expert, an individual may believe that the descriptions are specifically tailored to his or her personality and situation.

The B.E. influences the acceptance phenomenon, which describes the general tendency of humans towards accepting almost any feedback on their personality. B.E. is also known to promote the idea of subjective validation. Scholars believe that subjective validation is the tendency for people to accept an idea as being true if it is directed to them individually, and if it is of a positive nature (Psychology Concepts). In subjective validation, an individual is made to believe that two random events are to be related due to expectation or belief. For instance, when individuals are presented with astrological descriptions or when they read a horoscope, they eagerly look for a connection between what they are told and how they perceive their personalities.

It has been noted that when people hear a negative statement, they are not likely to apply it to themselves. Therefore, the B.E. works best for positive comments (Britannica.com). However, when presenting a negative description, the statements are cleverly structured to start with positive words, but generally, most statements are positive. The following list shows some statements that are used to describe an individual's characteristics or personality when they consult astrologers:

- Sometimes you spend a lot of energy and resources on projects that don't work out as planned.
- You would rather experience changes, and you don't like feeling limited in what you can accomplish.
- At times you can become so loud, friendly, and outgoing, but at other times you become so quiet, timid, and shy.
- When evaluating your capabilities, you are not overly harsh or very critical of yourself.
- You know that you have some weaknesses, but you try very hard to be a better person by overcoming your weaknesses.
- You have a deep desire to be liked and accepted by other people.

- You think independently, and you enjoy doing things in a unique way different from others.

- You are a disciplined and self-controlled individual on the outside, but you tend to be anxious and insecure on the inside.

- You believe that you are an independent thinker and do not easily accept other peoples' viewpoints without satisfactory facts.

- You prefer a degree of change and variety and you are not satisfied when you are faced with rules and restrictions.

- Sometimes you have major doubts wondering whether you have made the right decision or done the right thing.

- You think it is unwise to open up so much and to reveal yourself to other people.

- ⬚ You have a lot of unused potentials which you can turn to your advantage.
- ⬚ Sometimes you dream of attaining unrealistic expectations.
- ⬚ One of your major aims in life is security.

These are general statements that don't need any scientific criteria to prove that they apply to a specific individual.

Astrology and horoscopes make use of B.E. by convincing people that their description of them is highly individual and unique and could never apply to anyone else. Therefore, B.E. is manifested in response to general characterizations attributed to an individual which are perceived to be true. However, they are too vague and general, and they can apply to almost anyone.

Basically, the intent behind individuals claiming to have extraordinary powers is to use astrology and horoscopes to convince their clients to pay. To achieve their goal, these specialists employ B.E. to make people believe that they have an extraordinary ability to describe personalities. Innocently, individuals are eager to relate what they are told with the circumstances in their personal lives. What many ignore is that there is no scientific proof that these descriptions apply only to them as individuals. The appeal is on logical thinking rather than carefully evaluated and proven scientific facts. Astrology and horoscopes heavily rely on the Barnum Effect. One definition of astrology as we have earlier noted is that it is the study of the relationship between the position of the planets and events on earth. Horoscopy claims that at the time that a person is born, the positions of the planets, the Sun, and the Moon have a direct influence on that person's character. The location of the planets, the Sun, and the Moon are thought to affect a person's destiny. At the same time, astrologers believe that free will plays a significant role in an individual's life.

2.3 HEURISTICS AND THE METHODS OF ASTROLOGY

Heuristics are simple techniques adopted to seek immediate solutions to problems or reach a quick decision that though may not be optimal but solves an immediate problem. It invariably creates room for more investigations. An argument on astrology as a culturally applied heuristics will be considered here, but this should come after a basic understanding of the methods of astrology. An understanding of the methods of astrology will enable us understand more of how astrology works and is likely help us develop a curiosity as to how astrology came about its methods and seeming sophistications in the first place. It is this curiosity that the insights on astrology as a culturally transmitted heuristics will seek to subsequently offer an explanation for. This will also further prompt us on the discussion about the validity of the predictions as a way of confirming or refuting the scientific nature of these methods. We can then on our own objectively evaluate the believability of whatever valuables astrology offers, by weighing them on the scale of subsequent advancements in knowledge, inquisitorial methods and the trajectory of human civilization, which have altogether provided more progressive enlightenment on concepts, observations and theories from antiquity that were previously shrouded in mysteries or based on unaided observations.

Astrology has several predictive methods. An astrological chart is often used across the various methods and is constructed using such inputs as birth date, zodiac sign, aspect (i.e. the angular distance between the celestial bodies that apply in each case), the angle (e.g. the *Ascendant*) and any other important details depending on the method employed. The sequence of results is then analyzed, and based on this analysis a prediction of future likelihoods is made. Below are four major predictive methods used in astrology:

1. The Solar and Lunar Revolutions/Returns
2. The Progressions
3. The Transits
4. Horary Astrology

1. **<u>The Solar and Lunar Revolutions/Returns:</u>**

The solar return (SR) is the reading of the Sun's movement through the sky in a given year, until it reaches its natal placement, or where it was when the person, relationship or entity could be said to have been born. While the lunar return (LR) is a monthly reading of the instant moon and its movements in the sky until it returns to the exact position of birth. For the SR, a chart is cast with the precise day and time for any given year, and for the place or stage where a person, relationship, place, or project is, based on the significant date that marks their birthday. When the Sun's position in the return chart is exactly the same as in the natal chart, it is then interpreted as a new natal chart, and is valid for only one year. The arrangement of the planets in the course of these readings are used to also forecast events in the coming periods of the year, ranging from times of tensions to periods of harmony based on the converging points of the natal and return charts. Inquirers can then choose to align their thoughts and expectations at these various periods to the forecasts that they have been given.

2. **The Progressions:** Progressions are astrological charts that are moved forward on a sequence of one day for one year (*secondary progression*), or one degree for one year (*solar arc progression*). This ancient technique of late hasn't been as frequently used as it once was, because at the initial period of its use, Jupiter, Saturn, Uranus, Neptune and Pluto, known as the outer planets, were not known. The relevance of these outer planets (i.e. Jupiter through Pluto) have had to be factored in, and being that they do not reflect much movement because of their relative distance, astrologers sometimes seem to prefer other similar predictive methods, such as the use of transits which are close to progressions in form, to make their projections. Transits and SR techniques are

considered more proficient for use compared to progressions because astrologers observe that throughout a person's lifetime, the outer planets' positions will not change significantly, thus limiting the bandwidth of astrological readings. But this doesn't rule out the prominence of progressions, and the "aspects" derived from progressions in the inner planets have significant meanings. For instance a progressed Venus signals a period of much importance in areas of emotional, personal and creative interests, while those of Mercury and Mars point to changes in an environment of increased mental activity/travel/ or literary activity, and changes in a period of increased activity/enterprise/ or conflict respectively. So, progressions are commonly considered to be a relevant tool for the analysis of the personality's slow and deep evolution more in the psychological sense, than as a forecast of concrete events.

3. **The Transits:** Transits involve a method of interpreting the movements of planets passing through the constellations over a Natal chart with particular attention paid to changes in the signs, houses, aspects or angles that the transiting planet makes with the natal chart. It is then used to foresee the nature of major events as indicated by the astrological houses where the said aspects fall, and by the rulerships of the planets involved. Transits are more personally significant when they activate a natal fast-moving inner planet. Though astrologers pay high attention to the aspects formed by transiting outer planets because they remain longer on a given point, and their influences are thus said to deeply permeate the crucial points of the natal chart. Viewed from the Earth, and according to their orbit, the planets can move in transitory or even in retrograde motion to their initial position at a person's birth, indicating the completion of a cycle and the beginning of a new one. A lot of

astrologers enjoy the predictive techniques inherent in transits and believe that when coupled with the Solar Revolution method, it becomes a very powerful predictive tool.

4. **<u>Horary Astrology:</u>** Horary astrology is an ancient branch of astrology in which a chart is used to answer a precise question for the exact time and place where the question is asked. Horary astrology has its own strict system of interpretation in which the aspects of the moon are of strong importance and represented by the ruler of the sign in which the first house cusp falls. The prediction tells how the event or project will turn out according to the time the undertaking is initiated. The concept of planetary dignity is of importance to horary astrology both for the *essential dignity* and the *accidental dignity*. When a planet, for example Mars, is in Scorpio on the zodiac, it is considered to be a good Mars; on the contrary, Mars in Taurus signifies a bad Mars because it is in its

detriment and therefore in a weak state. Charts can also be turned to cast predictions for more remote variables such as where the querent (the inquirer) asks a question about his father's sibling, if the fourth house represents the father and the third house is for siblings, "turning the chart" could be used to make the predictions by counting three house from the fourth.

Many astrologers today seem to be shying away from making emphatic claims about predicting specific events in the future, they instead claim that astrology shows possible paths that lie ahead and only tells when potentials shown on a Natal chart are more likely to be prominent[28], whether in the positive or negative sense. The predictions, according to them, are subject to the free will of the individual who can counteract whatever fate is presented by his or her choices. By implication, the claim here is that astrology casts patterns in order to predict a trend of

[28] Jeff Mayo; Christine Ramsdale (1979). "*Teach Yourself Astrology*". Ntc Publishing Group, p.5.

possible circumstances, so as to guide, prepare or caution the querent.

The above identified methods aren't the only ways through which astrology makes its predictions, but they are well-known in the traditions of Western Astrology. Even if there are arguments as to a defective representation of methods here, an exhaustive listing of all the known methods of Astrology is outside the scope of this text. The essence of highlighting the predictive measures here mentioned is to show that astrology has some form of methodology; and that these methods operate on certain pre-existing theories that have been handed down over the centuries (though there are multiple variations and new infusions in their application); and also that there are important instruments and symbolic variables that are combined to make astrological predictions. These are the reasons for which curiosity as to the origination, justification and more importantly the efficacy of astrological methods and their underlying theories is necessarily reasonable. In the meantime, we can state from the foregoing that:

1. Astrology makes predictions. Whether these predictions are specific or have a lose generalization, the point is that they are predictions (e.g. your lost diamond ring will be found *or* there will be circumstances in your life that will teach you new lessons to mature you).

2. Astrology has theories. For example, there are theories relating to each of the "inner planets", and the "outer planets", the Sun, the Moon and the significance of their roles in the accuracy of predictions.

3. Astrology employs methods in reaching its predictions. Whether through the Returns, Transits, Progressions or other forms of methods, there are methods employed to arrive at its predictions.

4. Astrology uses instruments and symbolic variables in arriving at predictions. Such things as the Zodiac signs, Natal charts,

Houses, Date, Time, Place, the *Ascendant*, *Angles*, and *Aspects* are among the instruments and symbolized variables that astrology employs.

5. Astrology employs these various theories, methods, instruments and symbolized variables in an attempt to arrive at outcomes, representations or predictions that are products of a process and thus imply that they are credible intelligence or information of things to come. The very essence of its internal processes would seem to be to arrive at what it would consider credible and justifiable predictions that people can rely on in the explanation of social phenomena. This point reasonably follows from the foregoing, because outside of this deductible fact, there would be no reason in the first place for having to subject any inquiry to astrological processes. So, it goes without saying that astrology by its very posture claims that its predictions are credible, being products of a

credible process. Therefore, if there are established empirical lapses in its predictions, these are by relation an impugnment on the processes that produce the predictions.

It behoves that if astrology has methods, theories and instruments by which it arrives at its predictions, such predictions should be tested to prove their empirical worth and in turn validate the process or processes that produced them. Predictions that align consistently with observable data, by virtue of their consistency take on a scientific nature even if there aren't sufficient explanations yet behind the origin of their theories. As Thagard (1978) notes, there are proofs of mystical influences in Newtonian and Einsteinian breakthroughs, and modern chemistry has its roots in alchemy, hence the seemingly mystical wrap around a theory in his view doesn't preclude it from its scientific relevance; the greater challenges are in the inconsistencies and difficulties experienced in reconciling available data to its theoretical foundations and the credibility of the predictions made. Such challenges as how the precession of the equinoxes affects its zodiacal map, and the static nature of its explanatory power through the millennia remain really problematic concerns.

2.3.1 Astrology as a Culturally Transmitted Heuristics

Mark Hamilton (2015) in his response[29] to Genovese (2014) tries to offer an explanation for astrology as a culturally transmitted heuristics in a response to Genovese' critique[30] of Adel, Hossain and Johnson (2013)[31]. *Adel et al* set out to find out if there is any favored zodiac sign for celebrity births.

Adel *et al* (2013) in their study of 100, 200 and 300 celebrities and their zodiac signs, discovered that Aquarius had the highest frequency of celebrities at 14, 26 and 45, with a range of Pearson's correlation

---

[29] Hamilton M.A. (2015). "Astrology as a Culturally Transmitted Heuristic Scheme for Understanding Seasonality Effects: a Response to Genovese (2014)", *Journal of Comprehensive Psychology* Vol. 4 (7).

[30] Genovese, J.E.C. (2014). "A failed demonstration of sun sign astrology", *Journal of Comprehensive Psychology* Vol. 3 (16).

[31] Adel, M.M.; Hossain, S.F.; and Johnson .H. (2013). "Favored Zodiac for Celebrity Births", Journal of Social Sciences Vol. 9 (4).

coefficients at $r = .48$, $r = .48$, and $r = .59$, respectively. The study concluded that Zodiac birth signs and the number of celebrities were moderately related as shown by the correlation coefficients in the range of 0.50 to 0.60. Genovese (2013) however contends that the study was methodologically flawed, ascribing the positive effects to methodological artifacts, and proceeded to re-analyze the largest data of 300 celebrities used by Adel *et al*.

Genovese (2013) questions the use of Aries as the first listing of the Zodiac signs, stating that though there has been a culture of using Aries, there is no universally accepted order, and that with a rearrangement of the order of listing, the results were bound to be different. He also contends that there are other influences from social phenomena which the study leaves open that might be mistaken for astrology, such as relative age effects and season-of-birth effects. He criticizes the study for its lack of reference to other studies, and that it ignores the phenomenon of the precession of the equinoxes and its effect on the position of the sun in popular astrology. His re-analysis in one turn did place Aquarius at an r = .13, Aries at r = .59 and Pisces at r = .41 having run the analysis 12 times, with a new zodiac sign beginning each turn.

Hamilton (2015) observes that without the systematic deduction from observable facts that science can produce, the early civilizations of the Near East (i.e. the Egyptian, Babylonian, Greek and Roman civilizations) for instance were left to explain what they observed in nature with heuristics; the knowledge gained from this influenced their cultures in terms of successful farming; coping with flooding, infestation, or disease; and warfare. Derived from a Greek word that means "to discover", **heuristics** describe rules or methods that come from experience and which help people to solve problems, think things through, learn, discover, or gain understanding by speculating, guessing, evaluating possible answers or solutions, applying the process of elimination, or by trial and error. Hamilton explains that these heuristics from ancient civilizations also incorporated background assumptions about supernatural forces, including the effects that the planets and distant star clusters are believed to have on earthly events among other mythical beliefs; and it is this scheme of using heuristics that he says astrology originated from. Citing Eagly and Chaiken (1993), he states that there is a noted recognition of heuristics as a way of solving complex tasks when there are difficulties in following a systematic process to resolve such complexities. Hamilton's import of this reasoning is to explain the pervasive presence of astrology across global cultures, as a means of transmitting essential knowledge about the environment from one generation to another. In the course of these transmissions, myths were numinously imbedded and the Zodiacal signs emerged as a heuristic explanation of what were associated with the Zodiac symbols. Hence Hamilton holds the opinion of Smithers and Cooper (1978: p.240) that astrological predictions relating to personality and occupation, when aggregated across a vast number of observations at the societal level, may yield accurate predictions because they are the equivalent of historical folk wisdom about seasonality effects—which by implication are products of some sort of observation, no matter how crude.

Hamilton points out that, the sequence of sun signs that Adel, *et al.* (2013) used corresponds to increases in longitude within the celestial sphere beginning on March 20 at the equinox, which is when the amounts of daylight and night are approximately equal and is also the first point of Aries. As the first sign of the zodiac, Aries has an ecliptic longitude of 0° (covering 0°-30°, actually 0°-29.9°), while each of the 12 signs is described by 30° of ecliptic longitude up to Pisces the last sign, which culminates with an ecliptic longitude value of 330°. Hamilton emphasizes that the Adel, *et al* data showed a substantial linear correlation ($\beta = 0.59$, $p = .04$) between this Ecliptic Longitude Sequence (ELS) and celebrities-per-sign. Hamilton observes that Genovese (p. 1) misunderstood the arbitrariness that Adel *et al.* meant by assigning the number "1" to Aries, stating that it applied to the value of "1" assigned and not to the position of Aries on the zodiac, which in turn forms the foundation for Hamilton's position that the correlations in the Adel *et al* data may be more about seasonality (i.e. predictable changes that recur at regular intervals of a year in form of seasons) instead of distant zodiacal star clusters. In Hamilton's view, if astrology is therefore a heuristic scheme for explaining a people's observations of the complex relationship between seasonality effects and personalities, it shouldn't be dismissed, because when aggregated across a vast number of observations at the societal level, it may yield accurate predictions, since it is equivalent to the historical folk wisdom across societies about seasonality effects. He opines that these aggregate observations in turn can be the basis for collective folk wisdom linking seasonality to personality and behavior such as in occupations. He gives the impression that the prominence of astrology, especially sun sign astrology, is its explanation of sun signs as the center of human personality and self-concept, and in this wise has cultured the appetite of its enthusiasts over the years to regularly revisit the seasonal changes and turns that their personality types are open to, as the due course of their cultural inclinations in their perception of the effects that seasons have on humans.

But importantly, Hamilton's analysis takes into cognizance one of the contributions of Genovese' critique which is to the effect that the sun sign effect is indeed limited to the particular sequence that begins with Aries, tied to the March equinox, and that a rearrangement of this order by such other phenomena, like the precession of the equinox, will skew the results. In another vein, he states also that if Genovese is correct that relative age has been shown to produce differential mental and physical abilities within educational cohorts and that this might account for the observed correlation of .59 between sun sign ELS and celebrity, then the ELS could be dismissed as tangential to the important finding that relative age enormously increases the odds that a person will become famous. But after reviewing the outcomes of studies in this area, Hamilton proposes a different model in which case the ELS is used as a proxy for personality factors that mediate the effect of relative age on celebrity. In sum, the conclusion of Hamilton's response supports the empirical analysis of the Adel, *et al* study (2013) and also finds qualified support for the Genovese (2014) hypothesis that relative age does influence celebrity. He however canvasses his views within the modified context of the mediating role of seasonal birth heuristics instead of the supposed mystical effects of celestial objects on earthly events; and therefore called for more research in deeper dimensional studies on seasonal birth heuristics.

The relevance of the various arguments and analyses considered thus far in evaluating astrology is to the effect that the analyses afford us an opportunity to take a clinical view of astrology from the original value of its initial observatory explanation of the seasons and their roles in human affairs, up to the point of the extension of these roles to an order of zodiac sign traits that make predictive claims on seasonal circumstances in personal, relational, group and universal affairs. Heuristics are known to offer outlets to reach immediate goals in complex situations, but are also known to have serious limitations because they are not likely to be optimal; and may be imbued with cognitive biases, insufficient rationalization and inaccurate data. However, this doesn't take away the fact that they come from certain forms of observation and can be efficient means of reaching quick solutions. Observatory adaptations or theories can be said to have some form of scientific value, but only if those observations can be subsequently proven by available data. As we will see later on, Ptolemy's extensive explanation of the celestial was a product of observation, in which case he aligned initial beliefs and culturally held theories to observable information available at the time about the geocentric positioning of the earth at the center of the universe. Observations from the sky did seem like other planets revolved round the earth in circular motions. The fact that this turned out to be incorrect later on doesn't make it bad science (Heckert, 2011), it just means that more observable data and theory have falsified the initial claims and in fact Ptolemy's other postulation of circular orbits was sufficiently correct at the time. But even his theory of orbits which was partially correct, was not improved upon by Copernicus who invalidated the geocentric view through the postulation of the heliocentric model; instead, the orbit theory was modified by Kepler who used the original findings of Tycho to favor elliptical orbits over circular orbits even when Tycho himself didn't see this despite being the source of the data for the new theory. This is reflective of scientific progress.

These intricacies in improving on the understanding of observed phenomena is what makes it difficult to totally dismiss culturally transmitted explanations because their heuristic components may have some relevance. However, winnowing the chaff from the wheat and providing supporting data for such claims as astrology makes is important to determining its scientificity. More so, the adaptation to superior knowledge evidenced by empirical proof should lead to the enhancement of our observatory and explanatory power, so that old models of approaches in folk wisdom and reasoning are done away with in the face of new and better theories. The effect of the precession of the equinoxes as a ready instance ought to have had a form of modification on astrology, and the absence of this modification is a testament to the non-progressiveness of its enterprise and robs it of any scientific robe it might seek to wear.

This adds to the fact that astrology over the years has remained static in its explanation of the peculiar problems within its field, and keeps ascribing the theoretical basis for its practices to inexplainable (mystical) principles. Astrologers have done this with a cult-like religiosity as though to a sworn code of infallible tenets, the breach of which could spell doom to its practitioners. It is also easy to see from the foregoing analysis why astrology has a strong link to mythical traditions in its explanation of the world and the celestial. There is a strong similarity between the explanations offered by astrology and those offered by cultural myths such as are present in the *Zeus* Greek mythology, the *Yin & Yang* mythology of China or the *Obatala* mythology of the Yoruba people of West-Africa. The similarity astrology shares with these myths is the weakness in explanatory power, and the attribution of complex phenomena as the acts of mystical forces and powers, a deviation from the naturalistic philosophy of the sciences.

2.4 HOROSCOPE PREDICTIONS

A horoscope is an astrological forecast of a person's future based on the position of the planets and stars at the moment of someone's birth as cast on a chart. The following are used to cast charts:

Diagram 1: A Diagrammatic View of the Sun' Transit through the 12 Constellations

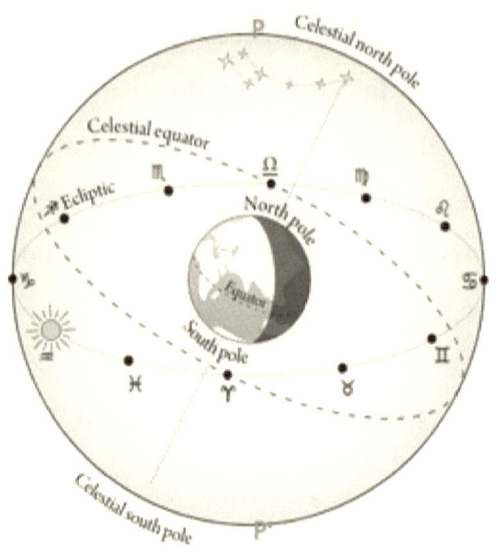

(a) <u>The Zodiac Signs and their Traits:</u> The zodiac is an imaginary belt in the heavens divided into twelve areas bearing the names of animals, human beings and mythological creatures, and at about 8^0 of the celestial latitude on the north and 8^0 on the south of the ecliptic, including in it the orbits of the planets. The twelve zodiac signs are affiliated with certain traits that are believed to be the primary defining qualities of human life born in such zodiacal time periods. Though the expression of these traits is influenced by other broad factors, such as the elements or the moon sign, but they essentially define the core characteristics of the four quadrants that astrology makes predictions for (i.e. individuals, relationships, groups, and the universal). Below are the twelve signs, the traits associated with them, and the applicable compatibility of signs in each case.

Table 2: Zodiac Signs, Traits and Compatibility

Zodiac Sign	Traits	Compatibility
Aries	Driven, Ambitious, Creative, Determined, Sociable, Humorous.	Gemini, Sagittarius, Aquarius, Capricorn and Pisces.
Taurus	Stubborn, Strong, Intelligent, Sympathetic, Loving.	Libra, Taurus, Cancer, Capricorn, Virgo and Pisces.
Gemini	Unpredictable, Creative, Open,	Gemini, Leo, Libra and

	Positive, Adaptable.	Aquarius.
Cancer	Traditional, Caring, Patient, Love to stay indoors.	Taurus, Leo, Virgo, Scorpio, Capricorn and Pisces.
Leo	Natural Leader, Brave, Strong, Headstrong, Loving, Generous.	Leo, Libra, Sagittarius, Cancer and Gemini.
Virgo	Perfectionist, Strong Memory, Instinctive, Organizational and Planning Skills, Team Player.	Virgo, Scorpio, Capricorn, Taurus and Cancer.
Libra	Introvert, Shy, Quiet, Trustworthy, Strong Sense of Justice.	Libra, Sagittarius, Leo, Taurus, Aquarius and Gemini.
Scorpio	Go-getter, Ambitious, Bold, Courageous, Self-confident, Decisive, Cool headed.	Capricorn, Pisces, Cancer and Virgo.
Sagittarius	Philosophical, Honest, Strong Work Ethic, Family Inclined.	Aquarius, Libra, Aries and Leo.
Capricorn	Very Intelligent, Patient, Determined,	Scorpio, Pisces, Virgo, Aries, Cancer and

	Diligent.	Taurus.
Aquarius	Exhibit Simplicity, are Honest, Loyal, Dependable, Smart, Independent, Reserved.	Aries, Gemini, Libra, Pisces, Sagittarius and Aquarius.
Pisces	Generous, Passionate towards others, Honest, Reserved.	Aries, Aquarius, Taurus, Cancer, Scorpio and Capricorn.

NB: Other astrological sources might include more qualities in the traits column above. They may use more adjectives to qualify them, or use alternative words in referring to them, but the above mentioned seem to be common among astrologers as associated with each of the signs.

(b) The Elements and their Significance: There are four elements that coincide with the classical four elements from antiquity and they are also used to mediate the reading of the astrological chart in formulating predictions. These elements are Fire, Air, Earth and Water; they are categorized into masculine and feminine gender with specialties.

Table 3: The Four Elements, Traits and Zodiac Signs

Gender Divisions	Elements	Traits	Zodiac Triplicities
Male (Extroverted)	Fire	Enthusiasm; drive to express self; faith. (confident, passionate, creative, can be temperamental)	Aries; Leo; Sagittarius
	Air	Communication; socialization; conceptualization. (social, communicative, intellectual, can be talkative)	Gemini; Libra; Aquarius
Female (Introverted)	Earth	Practicality; caution; comprehension of the material world. (practical, committed, stable, can be materialistic)	Taurus; Virgo; Capricorn
	Water	Emotion; empathy; sensitivity. (idealistic, security conscious, intuitive, can be easily overwhelmed)	Cancer; Scorpio; Pisces

(c) <u>The Moon Sign:</u> The moon sign is thought to be the actual reflection of the hidden self or inner self. In essence, while the sun sign projects outward traits, the moon sign reveals the inner traits.

(d) <u>Determine the Ascendant/Rising Sign and the House:</u> This is the sign and degree seen to be ascending towards the Eastern horizon at birth, beginning at 9 0'Clock, which shows the person's ascendant at birth, and progressing in an anticlockwise manner to reveal the houses in gradual succession. At each 30-degree interval in this reverse movement is a house that is dominated by its corresponding Zodiac. The Ascendant, is believed to have great importance in how a person is reflected or expresses him/herself outwardly, both at birth and subsequently.

Table 4: The Astrological Houses

1. 1st House (Aries)— House of Self.

2. 2nd House (Taurus)— House of Value

3. 3rd House (Gemini)— House of Communications.

4. 4th House (Cancer)— House of Family

5. 5th House (Leo)—House of Pleasure

6. 6th House

8. 8th House (Scorpio)— House of Reincarnation

9. 9th House (Sagittarius)— House of Philosophy

10. 10th House (Capricorn)— House of Social Status

11. 11th House (Aquarius)— House of Friendships

12. 12th House (Pisces)— House of Undoing

(Virgo)— House of Health	
7. 7th House (Libra)— House of Partnerships	

The question still remains "how did astrology come by its theories?" In the course of putting this study together, there was great difficulty in discerning sufficient harmony in the astrological body of knowledge available; for instance, while many astrologers do not use the outer planets (i.e. Jupiter, Saturn, Uranus, Neptune and Pluto) at all in their predictions, others consider them vital in getting certain other mediating variables, and yet still, some other astrologers include asteroids in their readings. It is therefore difficult to ascertain whether these practices are supposed to help in getting more accurate predictions. And if so, whose is more accurate? Is there enough data to assess the authenticity of any such claims? Interestingly, it raises doubts, if it isn't a disservice to astrology itself to lump all these practices under one umbrella, with the undefined expanse of arbitrary inputs, considering how much this can affect any progress that sections of its practitioners may want to make in improving the accuracy of the broad craft. Astrology seems more disorganized than it is projected.

The information provided in this chapter was aimed at relaying sufficient—though by no means exhaustive—information on the origins of astrology, the nature of its social influence, its methods, its theories, and the instruments that govern its predictions and practice. This will be a useful background as we progress in the text.

So far, we have seen that astrology had a pervasive presence across the major civilizations and cultures of the world as an attempt to explain the relationship between heavenly bodies and seasonal changes, and in the same vein extended the construction of a similar causal relationship between celestial bodies and events in personal, interpersonal, group and universal human experiences. The names of the zodiac signs as they are, can be traced to myths and legends surrounding deities, animals and other symbolized characters. Apart from the impelling needs faced in antiquity by such civilizations like the Egyptian and the Babylonian empires, which fuelled their leaning towards interpreting celestial signs for sustenance purposes—such as agriculture, preparation for the demands of the different seasons and war—we also observed the impact of Barnum Effect in reinforcing beliefs and trends in modern societies as a part of the influences in today's social leanings towards astrology. The heightened complexities of human life today in the midst of rapid globalization, fast-paced economic realities, strains in social connections and a multiplicity of demands, makes it easy to see how a person's perception of being addressed on a personal level by astrologers, and the reinforcement of vague and general descriptions thought to apply personally, can whip up followership that catches a flamboyant spread in societal life.

The points made under astrology as a culturally transmitted heuristics, was to stress three important points. The first being to contextualize the emergence of astrology in the explanation of phenomena and its transmission from generation to generation as a heritage of ancient civilizations. The second point was to state that astrology's umbilical cord are still tied to the mythological content of ancient civilizations, which is evident in the mystical affiliations inherent in its explanation of its foundational theories. And the third point is to show the limitation astrology faces in the static nature of its explanatory power as it relates to its problems in interpreting the world, a weakness that the deliberations on heuristics further revealed, since much of the contributions came from scholarly efforts in the field of Psychology, a more recent discipline that has no doubt progressively expanded the bounds of its explanations.

CHAPTER THREE
THE SCIENTIFIC TEST

As has been noted in chapters one and two above, there are characteristics that a scientific field must have for it to qualify as a science. It was also observed that astrology was initially regarded as a science until the 17th century when its scientific standing began to be more openly disputed by prominent scientists, some of whom were themselves originally astrologers. They began to separate the pure observation of the characteristics, properties and interactions of celestial phenomena and their cosmological effects (astronomy), from the interpretations of the constellations and their direct link to domestic human affairs and human destiny (astrology). Astronomy has been defined as the science that encompasses the study of all extraterrestrial objects and phenomena[32]. It includes the study of such celestial bodies as the planets, stars (including the sun and the moon), asteroids, and other forms of "matter" in space.

---

[32] *"Astronomy"*. Encyclopaedia Britannica (2019).

Astronomy has become a prominent field of science with several specialized branches such as Astrophysics (which is in certain contexts used interchangeably with Astronomy), Solar astronomy, Astrobiology, Planetary science, Astrochemistry, Galactic astronomy etc. It is one of the oldest natural sciences in the world, and the development of a fundamental understanding of the universe through astronomy is still in progress because as we have seen in recent phases of its development, astronomers have had to review their ideas about the overall shape, age, and contents of the Universe. The wisdom adopted here, is to consider the factors by which astronomy has acquired its scientificity as against the unscientific methods of astrology, in order to strike an objective contrast between the two fields which were once conjoined but have successfully undergone a surgery of separation. Interestingly, they do not share in constituent features the identificatory semblance of identical twins save in name where both share the prefixal "astro" (*astro*-nomy ‖↔‖ *astro*-logy), and the shared use of certain terminologies, indicating their common origin of enquiry into the world of the celestial, but with no further similarities as to the scientificity of their individual ventures.

3.1 THE WAYS OF SCIENCE

Paul A. Heckert, (Ph.D.) states that "Scientific methodology uses experimental and observational data to test hypotheses, models or theories. To qualify as scientific, these hypotheses, models, or theories must be subject to being proven wrong by observable data. They must be falsifiable. When data and theoretical models disagree, scientists should always modify the theoretical models to make them agree with the data"[33]. The above statements by Heckert, point to the fundamental character of science and scientific knowledge; it doesn't necessarily mean that every scientific claim is essentially accurate at the

[33] Paul A. Heckert, (September 5, 2011). "The History of Astronomy as an Example of Scientific Methodology". *Decoded Science,* Copyright © 2019 · Magazine Pro Theme on Genesis Framework.

outset, what it does connote is that any theory that is propounded or being tested must be in consonance with empirical data gathered during verification, and where there is a proven disparity between a hypothesis, model or theory and the gathered data, then such hypothesis, model or theory must be modified to conform to the available data and then subjected to another test. This is what is called falsifiability and is a cornerstone of the scientific method. The object or phenomenon that is the focus of a scientific enquiry or process must be such as can be perceived by the senses, or where they are not visible to the unaided eyes, are proven by scientific instruments. Thus, claims to extrasensory phenomena which aren't verifiable through scientific instruments, or by empirical consistency are not considered by the science community as part of science.

Scientists through various instruments and means ascertain that an object has properties such as atoms, molecules, size, temperature and density among other things to ensure that such an object actually exists and to eliminate the uncertainties of subjective claims that can undermine the credibility of new findings. A theory is a plausible or scientifically acceptable general principle or body of principles offered to explain phenomena [34]. A theory implies a greater range of evidence and greater likelihood of truth than a hypothesis. A law on the other hand, differs from a theory in that a theory gives explanations as to why a phenomenon operates in a certain way, while a law states a prediction of what would happen under specific circumstances. A scientific Law is a universal statement about a phenomenon based on empirical observation.

From the foregoing, we see that scientists primarily observe the universe, formulate questions, try to answer those questions from more observations or experiments, after which hypotheses are formulated for testing. A hypothesis is a tentative explanation of an observed phenomenon and is often called a scientific guess; it must make predictions that

---

[34] Merriam Webster Dictionary (2019).

can be tested by experiments to determine its validity or otherwise. A hypothesis which in the course of an experiment is at variance with emergent data can be modified to a new hypothesis which is then then tested or retested until it becomes stable. When a hypothesis has undergone several tests and has sufficient proof to support it, it may become accepted as a **theory,** and this means that it has been accepted as being able to repeatedly produce a particular outcome under specific conditions and thus very likely to be true. A hypothesis that has become a theory has proven to be correct over and over again and is accepted as a fact or theoretical fact until disproved by new findings or theories. Scientists have also found that natural phenomena interact only in specific ways and these interactions are what are stated as laws. A physical law can be either mathematically or conceptually expressed, and examples are: (i) $F = Gm_1m_2/r^2$ (mathematical expression of the Law of Gravity), and (ii) the law of conservation of energy which states that the total amount of energy in any isolated system remains constant, and cannot be created or destroyed, although it may change forms.

Science has a culture that members of the scientific community have developed to engender credibility, trust and information sharing. New findings are discussed through formal and informal platforms, are presented at conferences, published in refereed journals and are sometimes given to other scientists to scrutinize. Since scientists freely open their works to the scrutiny of other scientists, the reputation or trustworthiness of a scientist doesn't come in the way of repeat research, repeat experiments and verification of a scientific claim. This is why scientific fraud has been rare in its occurrence because misrepresentations or mistakes will easily be detected along the line. The motivation for contribution to knowledge, for discoveries and for learning about the natural world is the driving force over and above monetary gains. It involves laborious routines, painstaking consistency, diligence, consultation and reviewing of existing knowledge, series of fact checks, standard methodology, peer reviews, modeling, logical reasoning, data analysis, data relevance, proper referencing and publication of findings. To state with equanimity in the face of all these requirements that astrology is a science would require more than just a wish, or one or two papers or experiments. It would require a logical, consistent and thoroughly proven natural explanation for its claims, subjected to repeated tests by any group of scientists anywhere. These are the issues which astrology contends with that its previous ally astronomy has been able to surmount. We now take a closer look.

3.2 ASTROLOGY, SCIENCE AND CONTRADICTIONS

The following attributes do not represent an exhaustive list, but are reflective of the key features of the scientific process, and they include: observation, hypothesis, falsifiability, naturalism (i.e. solely resorting to natural means of explaining natural phenomena), predictability, empirical testability, experiments, repeatability, objective skepticism, data analysis, credit citation, publication, peer review, theory acceptance, application, and adoption of new findings. In view of this, it is apposite to test the conformity of astrology to these attributes and in the same vein test the conformity of any other known science, so that a contrastive analysis can shape our perception of the two fields. The known science adopted here as earlier indicated is astronomy.

In earlier times, a mixture of superstitious speculations and actual findings dotted the use of celestial knowledge which was considered as one of the Seven Liberal Arts; so that Kings had in their courts, advisers which they consulted on celestial matters to determine whether to go to war at a certain time based on the positioning of the celestial bodies, or what season they were, in the calendar of celestial movements. And being that at this time both disciplines hadn't been separated, the resources allotted from the palace funded more discoveries in celestial knowledge, and this mutually benefitted the activities of pure inquisitorial scholarship on the one hand, and the speculative theorizing of the celestial on the other hand. *Astronomia* was a term often used to jointly refer to the combined activities of both practices in Medieval Europe, though there are also evidences of the Latin word *Astrologia* used for both; and it was difficult to distinguish knowledge that came from scientific findings and that which came from the speculative theories of its art. To divide between both fields, the prominent figures from their past, and their vital works, one could say observations which were associated with the knowledge of the physics of celestial objects would point to the scientific branch; while predictions about social relations based on the positioning of celestial objects would point to the speculative branch.

Another unique characteristic they differ in is the philosophy of naturalism; and this implies that while science seeks a logical and empirical explanation of phenomena strictly within the bounds of the natural, astrology makes explanations that do not show natural causes or explanation. Thus, we can trace ideas that stay within natural explanations of causes and effects to Astronomy as they have been so adopted by it; while ideas without natural causes can be traced to Astrology, as Astrology has adopted and stuck with them. A good example is how astronomers identify with Ptolemy's *Almagest,* while astrologers identify with Ptolemy's *Tetrabiblos*—both treatises from the same author, but different in character. By the 17th century, known as the Age of Reason, they both began to branch out separately until they were completely separated by the 18th century. One area in which this shows itself is in the geocentric character that Astrology still carries till today, while Astronomy has gone even beyond the heliocentric discovery, and has adopted the view that the universe actually has no center and is constantly expanding. They share similarities in their celestial interests, their value for the interconnectivity within the cosmos, and the use of some terms like the ecliptic, latitude, longitude, constellations (astrology focuses on 12 constellations, while Astronomy says there are 88 of them) among others. To proceed in this chapter, the contrast between astronomy and astrology will be subsumed under three headings:

(i)   The Test of Falsifiability

(ii)   The Test of Theoretical Acceptability

(iii)   The Test of Natural Empiricism

3.2.1 The Test of Falsifiability

Science has been described as a self-correcting process for acquiring knowledge, with many mechanisms for detecting errors. The first challenge with Astrology is the posture of its perpetual inerrancy and the static adoption of its ancient tenets despite new discoveries. Science has always proven itself to be an endeavor that is subject to new discoveries and is in this wise willing to adopt new found knowledge. Once a new theory has been thoroughly proven, science altogether drops any inconsistent theory, or modifies the inconsistencies in the old theory to align with the new knowledge. A case in point is the idea of the geocentric world view, which dominated the beliefs of the ancient world, stating that the earth was the center of the universe and that the sun and the moon revolved around the earth. Claudius Ptolemy who was one of the greatest astrologers and astronomers of history, had sought to explain the earth's position in the universe and had postulated that the universe was geocentric, i.e. that the earth was the center of the universe. His view was the predominant view in the astrological and astronomical spheres until the theoretician Nicolaus Copernicus, who like Aristarchus of Samos, formulated a different model that placed the sun at the center of the universe, postulating that the earth orbits around the sun. Subsequent discoveries proved this new theory to be true and today, actual photographs from space clearly show that the earth in conjunction with other planets orbit around the sun. Astronomy while appreciating the initial contributions of Ptolemy, did not however fail to admit the more correct position of Copernicus, and even greater accuracies that have since been discovered; however, today Astrology essentially retains its geocentric views and puts man at the significant center of the universe, extending this assertion to the movements of the planets as an organized system of interconnected activities designed for man's purposes on earth. Though astrologers argue that the essentiality of their geocentric view is because the earth is the center of observation, which should not be taken to imply that it is the center of the universe and that ancient astrology never completed a sun cycle in one day, as a matter of fact it was cast in yearly cycles[35]. The difficulty in this argument however is that the leading astrological thinkers upon which much of western astrology has depended postulated actual theories of a geocentric world from which astrology gleaned and for which it has made no considerable effort to re-explain so as to fit into new knowledge.

While there are arguably no other planets proven to sustain life, however the discovery of several celestial systems by astronomy has logically prevented it from reaching these kinds of conclusions,

---

[35] Saravana Kumar .G. (2014). "*Astrology—Heliocentric or Geocentric Model*". Retrieved from https://innovativeastrosolutions.wordpress.com/2014/04/2 6/astrology-heliocentric-or-geocentric-model/comment-page-1/

as there are constant expeditions to other planets to make more discoveries. Astrology is however not able to make any natural or empirical explanations for its views and still constructs its natal charts and horoscope predictions based on <u>the movement of the sun and the moon within the twelve constellations, claiming that the sun spends an equal amount of time within each constellation.</u> As mentioned earlier on, there is evidence that a 13th constellation had hitherto been discovered from Babylonian times, but was suppressed because it would have altered their adopted yearly calendar projections and distorted their previous claims. While scientists have adopted greater measures to strengthen the credibility of the scientific method of proof, astrology has struggled to sustain its credibility by insisting on the perpetual consistency of its ancient theories and predictions through its posture of inerrancy.

This discrepancy in approach by these two disciplines is sufficient grounds in itself to separate the nature of their character in terms of what is scientific and what is speculative/mystic.

Falsifiability as a principle makes it important for science to seek to disprove a hypothesis or an existing theory until it is able to consistently stand after being subjected to several processes. To take another example, the Earth in addition to rotating on its axis (giving us the routine change in day and night) and orbiting the Sun (giving us our yearly changes in season), has been discovered to have another more gradual motion that was quite unknown for long and isn't even popular in today's parlance, unlike the popularity which the daily rotation and the yearly revolution have. The earth's axis tips around in a circle, like the tipping of a spinning top. The Earth's tipping motion is called precession and slowly completes a full circle a little over 25,000 years. As a result of precession, the Earth's axis will point in a different direction over some good number of years; this explains why the current star on the earth's North Pole, i.e. Polaris, was not always the one above our planet's north pole, it was formerly Thuban 3,000 years ago.

This implies that the constellations where the sun is said to traverse against the background of stars in a given month also changes; and if the full circle of precession takes roughly 25,000 years and the zodiac is divided into 12 signs, it follows that precession tips the Sun over by one sign in about every 2,000 years or so, so that someone born on August 1 some 2,000 years ago and considered by astrologers to have the Sun sign Leo definitely today is in the constellation Cancer, but astrologers are fixed to the Ptolemic codifications and will not as much as rotate the positions of the constellations in light of the new knowledge, this trumps its scientific claims. The current constellations in use are definitely incorrect, this is because they are outdated and factually proven to be altered, leaving any current predictions by horoscopes as fallacious speculations steeped in the unbendable traditions of ancient mystical theories as against the scientific orientation people have about them. Astrology doesn't pander to the falsifiability principle which organized science has adopted, this contradiction and misalignment certainly calls to question its scientific claims and makes its posturing as a science at best a failed attempt to acquire the credibility often associated with the sciences.

Paul R. Thagard[36] in his arguments about the pseudoscientific nature of astrology, argues that falsifiability alone is not sufficient grounds to say a field of study isn't scientific because falsifiability is only relevant when a new theory comes to challenge an existing theory, and that many scientific theories themselves are severally modified by auxiliary hypotheses in order to be retained and not be falsified. He restates the positions of Popper (1959) that no observation can guarantee falsification until there is a new theory that succeeds; and since what is scientific today may become a pseudoscience tomorrow, it only remains scientific until faced with a new theory. He was implying here that the history of astrology itself may favor its initial scientific reputation since it was at some point the only explanatory field in terms of

---

[36] Paul R. Thagard, (1978) "Why Astrology Is A Pseudoscience". *Philosophy of Science Association Journal*, Vol. 1, pp. 223-234.

the aspect of the universe and human affairs that it dealt with at the time, just as it is with other sciences until a new theory overturns the existing theory. He however points out that one thing that makes astrology a pseudoscience is its static nature after these number of years, and that alternative explanations for instance in psychology, in regards to many similar aspects astrology deals with, keep expanding in their explanations and problem-solving attempts unlike astrology. The point of Thagard on falsifiability not being an immutable standard for disproving a subject from being a science is well noted, it however does not derogate from the initial arguments presented here, and that when a theory is challenged by new facts, data or theories, but maintains its original theoretical stand, it assumes a posture of inerrancy even in the face of contrary data and by this inclination loses its scientific character.

3.2.2 The Test of Theoretical Acceptability

Thagard (1978) posits that every scientific field has unresolved problems and questions and that astrology shouldn't be an exception. It shouldn't therefore be put off as a pseudoscience simply because it isn't able to reconcile the disparities in its theories and majority of the data gathered to ascertain them. Reference will be made to this as we progress, however at the fundamental level, Thagard notes that there are unresolved theoretical differences even amongst astrologers, with no harmonized theoretical approach for resolving them. Fraknoi (2012)[37] also observes that astrologers themselves seem to disagree on the most fundamental issues of their craft: whether on how to account for the precession of the Earth's axis, or to determine how many planets and other celestial objects should be included in determining their charts, or which personality traits should go with which cosmic phenomena, all points to a lack of harmony in theory. The poser then is if astrology is a science, as

---

[37] Andrew Fraknoi (2012) *"An Astronomer Looks at Astrology"*. The Universe at Your Fingertips
• Astronomical Society of the Pacific.

its proponents claim, why are its practitioners not converging on a consensus theory after thousands of years of gathering data and refining its interpretation?

Both astronomy and astrology make predictions. While the later makes predictions from astrological charts based on ancient theories and deduced from celestial interactions within the zodiac, the former bases its initial and final predictions on a known method cycle that has been consistently enhanced over the years but has retained its basic characteristics. It starts with a hypothesis, after which the prediction is further observed, experimented and where necessary modified and retested until it is able to stand as a theory (itself an explanation of the tested prediction) or discarded. A brief comparison of the theoretical process of both will be considered here.

(i) **<u>The Theoretical Process and Proof</u>**: Hypatia of Alexandria was a female philosopher, mathematician and Astronomer who taught mathematics and astronomy in Alexandria and was the first female to make substantial contributions to mathematics. She lived in the 4th century in what was predominantly a man's world and was stoned to death by an angry mob in a time of religious strife. It is said that most of her works are lost and that those being passed around are fictitious, however a unique analysis she gives of the scientific method as published by the Colorado University is interesting. She once taught her students how the developments in astronomy had contributed to the scientific method and its theoretical approach to explaining phenomena. Her model[38] shows the relations between hypotheses, predictions and measurements in the formulation of theories and is represented in the diagram below:

---

[38] Laboratory for Atmospheric and Space Physics, University of Colorado (LASP). *"Hypatia Astronomy"* http://lasp.colorado.edu/~bagenal/1010/SESSIONS/5.ScienceAstronomy.html . Retrieved 3rd April 2019.

From our previous discussions and the above diagram, we see that the scientific method starts with a hypothesis, and requires that from such a hypothesis specific predictions are made about what are to be the expected outcomes of a process under specific conditions. It is then subjected to what Hypatia refers to as measurement, to repeatedly verify the hypothesis and the predictions made under the specified conditions—and where necessary, further trialed under diverse conditions—before it makes its final transition to the theory level. If the observations and data collected point to the fact that the hypothesis is incorrect, the hypothesis is then to be modified or thrown out altogether. As a hypothesis gains more and more backing in the form of new experiments and measurements that support it, it gradually becomes a theory or a law, which itself can either be invalidated or modified later on by a more accurate theory. Hypathia notes that in this sense, a scientific theory is not "just a guess", but is something that has an enormous amount of evidence behind it, because in reality, scientific progress is not made in such a simple and straightforward manner—there are "red-herrings", "U-turns and blunders along the way". The key point here is that theories in a science, e.g. astronomy, emerge from a thorough and repeated process of verified data and empirical evidence that support the claims in the theory, but the case with astrology seems different.

If consideration is given to the position earlier adopted by Hamilton (2015) that being a culturally transmitted heuristics, astrology may yield accurate predictions as the equivalent of historical folk wisdom about seasonality effects acquired over time, then a comparative analysis of the acceptance or rejection of folk wisdom based on scientific discoveries should be factored in. Seeing that most theories developed in less sophisticated times have been reviewed under the scrutiny of better scientific instruments, so that those that were inaccurate by virtue of new empirical data have been replaced by new theories, and those that stood the test of proof have remained, albeit with more robust explanations. It is questionable why the theories of astrology have not gone through any deliberate reviews if not to enhance them, but to at least improve on their explanatory power in relation to problems associated with astrology and the justification of the emergence of the said theories. Much more, what happens when its predictions do not turn out to be correct as it has been in several cases? Will the problem be said to be with the data? Or will it be inaccuracy on the part of the astrologer? Or will it be the theories upon which the prediction was made? These questions are perplexing. Why do many results of tests carried out under the relevant specifications not consistently turn out well? Yet there are no modifications whatsoever to accommodate such tendencies, neither are there attempts made at that time or subsequently to give coherent explanations? Is it not possible that much of the scanty incidences of supporting data are just what they are—incidences? The adopted position here is that astrology has no interactive cycle of theory, prediction and empirical measurement, what we have is a one-way top-to-bottom progression that is repeated over and over again regardless of whether the results are verifiable or not because the theories are deified with a supposed inerrancy and infallible ancientness. So while Thagard (1978) is right that all fields of endeavors have unresolved problems, the real issue is with astrology's static nature. Below is a diagram of the theoretical progression in astrology.

Diagram 3: The Astrological Theory Cycle

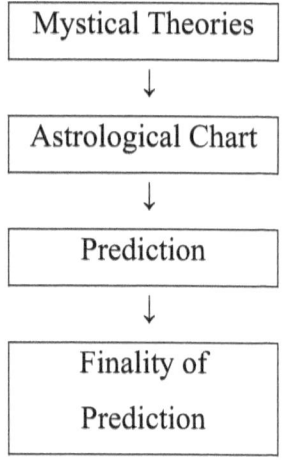

Mystical Theories
↓
Astrological Chart
↓
Prediction
↓
Finality of Prediction

(ii) **<u>Static Theories:</u>** The scientist **Hipparchus** was a Greek astronomer and mathematician who made fundamental contributions to the advancement of astronomy as a mathematical science[39]. Hipparchus carried out accurate measurements with precise instruments such as the astrolabe, made a catalog of about 850 stars and measured their relative magnitudes. It was Hipparchus who discovered the **precession of the equinoxes**. The establishment of this discovery had great implications for astronomy and ought to have had for astrology being that at the time of this discovery, astronomy and astrology were still very much seen as one and the same, and without clear delineations. However as it has turned out, this hasn't happened even after over two millennia of this discovery, and the closest guess must be because of the implications such a

[39] Britannica 2019.

discovery will have on the authenticity of astrological claims over the years. Several references have already been made to the precession of the equinoxes in this text, the prime focus here will be to contrast the static nature of astrology even in the face of new and credible information, as against the more scientific character of astronomy which has over the years progressed in its adaptation to new knowledge and more comprehensive explanations of the universe. A classic illustration and analysis is offered by Heckert (2011)[40] in his explanation of the place of the scientific method in the growth of astronomy. His presentation is quite a graphic appreciation of scientific progress and has been captured here because of its narrative simplicity and the

---

[40] Paul A. Heckert, Ph.D. is a professor of physics and astronomy at Western Carolina University.

historical hindsight it offers. Here is what Heckert has to say[41]:

"Since the dawn of humanity, people have observed the night sky. Ancient cultures observed various motions in the sky including the relative motions of the planets against the stellar backdrop. To scientifically explain these observed motions, ancient Greeks, culminating with Ptolemy, developed the first scientific models. Ptolemy's model was geocentric. It placed Earth at the center of the cosmos. Greek aesthetic ideas favored circles and spheres as perfect geometric figures. The ancient Greeks thought that celestial objects must be perfect spheres moving in circular paths at a uniform speed. All celestial objects therefore moved around Earth in paths consisting of combinations of uniform circular

[41] Paul A. Heckert, (September 5, 2011). "The History of Astronomy as an Example of Scientific Methodology". *Decoded Science,* Copyright © 2019 · Magazine Pro Theme on Genesis Framework. Retrieved at www.decodedscience.org/the-history-of-astronomy-as-an-example-of-scientific-methodology/2867 . Retrieved 3rd April 2019, 6:05pm.

motions. To develop the final Greek model, Ptolemy modified details of previous versions so that the predicted positions of planets and other celestial objects would agree with observed positions. The Ptolemaic model was therefore good science because it changed the model to conform to the data. The model's predictions agreed with the observations of planetary positions [to] within the accuracy of the observations available at the time. The fact that it later turned out to be incorrect does not make Ptolemy's model bad science. In the 16th century, Copernicus proposed an alternative heliocentric model that placed the Sun at the center of the solar system. Copernicus however continued with the Greek tradition of uniform circular motion. In Copernicus's model the planets orbited in circular orbits around the Sun, so the Copernican model was no more accurate than the Ptolemaic model in predicting positions of planets. Copernicus was motivated by aesthetics in science is often underappreciated. To decide which competing model was better, astronomers needed more accurate data.

Tycho Brahe supplied these data. Tycho spent his entire career collecting data on positions of celestial objects with an unprecedented accuracy. When Tycho died, Johannes Kepler used Tycho's data to modify the Copernican heliocentric model. Most notably, Kepler's model used elliptical orbits rather than the traditional circular orbits. Why? Tycho's data demanded the modification. Kepler was unable to find a combination of circular orbits that agreed with Tycho's accurate data, so he modified the model to use elliptical orbits. Elliptical, but not circular, orbits agreed with Tycho's more accurate data. Kepler also devised his three laws of planetary motion. Newton later devised the laws of motion that explained Kepler's laws. In the early 20th century, Einstein's special and general theories of relativity modified Newton's laws for certain situations in which Newtonian predictions did not agree with data. Notice that the various steps in scientific methodology are incorporated into the development of astronomy. Specifically better data falsified the models, compelling astronomers to modify and improve their understanding of the cosmos".

This interesting view presented by Heckert is one of the reasons astronomy has gained scientific ascendancy over astrology. It forms the basis for an earlier statement in this text that it is possible to trace back to antiquity a thread of consistent scientific efforts more attributable to astronomy, and which astronomy has adopted into its body of knowledge; while by the same token, it is equally possible to delineate the thread of abstractions, mystical assertions and inaccurate data through antiquity, much of which astrology seems to stick with and has identified itself more with. Another case in point is the actual width of each constellation within the ecliptic, added to the discovery that the sun actually passes through thirteen constellations instead of twelve, a long recognized fact even in Babylonian, Greek and Roman times[42]. The Babylonians had a 12-

---

[42] Peters, Christian Heinrich Friedrich and Edward Ball Knobel (1915). *"Ptolemy's Catalogue of Stars: A Revision of the Almageist"*. Carnegie Institution of Washington.

month lunar calendar, and so they chose the initial twelve constellations and divided the year up evenly as the transit periods of the sun within each constellation. The thirteenth constellation is called *Ophiuchus* (interpreted from Greek to mean *"serpent-bearer"*) and it interjects with its tail end between Scorpio and Sagittarius—this in itself throws a spanner in works of the sun's transits through the constellations because the interference of *Ophiucus* ought to bear on the transit of the sun. Evidence shows that the physical constellations actually take up varying widths of the ecliptic, so that for instance Virgo occupies five times as much longitude as Scorpio, thus making the current zodiacal constellation of astrology a static and misleading abstraction. These inconsistencies portray the craft of astrology and its processes as abstractive mechanisms that do not rely on anything that is actual.

Being an abstraction, it is obvious that it operates in a separate contextual realm, only using its reference to the celestial bodies as a way of gaining some sort of tangibility, when in actual fact its predictions and practices are premised on intangible, vague and abstruse theories, steeped in an arcane mysticism that is at the heart of its theoretical claims. It seems more akin to an esoteric art with all the trappings of inaccessible theories, expertise and sophistry of divination.

Apart from the points so far raised on the theoretical weaknesses of astrology, the summary provided by Thagard (1978) in proving the theories of astrology as pseudoscientific are apposite and they are that :

1. It has been less progressive than alternative theories over a long period of time, and faces many unsolved problems. Astrology has faced significant anomalies over a long period of time and developments in Psychology are offering better explanations and expanding the space of alternatives in such a short time compared to astrology.

2. The community of practitioners makes little attempt to develop the theory towards solutions of the problems, shows no concern

for attempts to evaluate the theory in relation to others, and is selective in considering confirmations and disconfirmations.

(iii) **Theoretical Inconsistencies:** If astrology were to make other claims outside of the scientific and insist on their relevance to human life or the universe, it is well within its right as an endeavor to do so, in so far as it sticks with those claims. Though this won't preclude it from the criticisms of skeptics or the uninitiated, however, resorting to scientific claims in order to enhance its believability and authenticity, brings it within the purview and scrutiny of the scientific community. Dean, Lopston, Kelly and seven others have identified various theoretical inconsistencies which have over the years been associated with astrology, and in an updated publication by *Astrology and Science* some of the theories were highlighted and some of them include [43]:

(a) <u>Spiritual Theories</u>: Some of these spiritual theories could be found in works by astrologers such as Alice Bailey (1951, based on the seven rays), Charles Carter (1968, based on the zodiac as the pathway of the soul), Alan Leo (1913, based on karma and reincarnation), Dane Rudhyar (1969, based on actualization of potentialities), and Robert Schmidt (1990, based on the Greek principles of the One and the Many). These theories explain astrology as relating to the soul and put it within the spiritual domain, but the challenge is that astrology doesn't stay just within spiritual explanations because it is also applied to inanimate things such as ships, companies, countries etc. Except there are arguments that inanimate things also have souls—which will itself require empirical

---

[43] Dean, Lopston, Kelly and seven others, "Theories of Astrology: A Comprehensive Survey", first published in *Correlation* 1996, 15(1), pp.17-52 and updated by *Astrology and Science*. Available at: http://www.astrology-and-science.com/a-theo2.htm .

proof—it is easy to see that astrology makes wide claims that are in one breath spiritual in context, yet it also conjects beyond purely soulish or spiritual things. This creates a difficulty of ambivalence for a scientific theory, particularly when it is short of credible explanations.

(b) <u>Theories Based on the Physical</u>: There are two initially identified physical explanations that were popular among astrologers, i.e. the explanation by Charles Muses (1919-2000), a mathematician and philosopher, and Arthur Young (1905-1995), founder of the Institute for the Study of Consciousness. Muses's explanation based on his book *Destiny and Control in Human Systems* (1985) talks of the structure of time, in which lines, circles and helixes in time express the relationship between macrocosm and microcosm. Young's explanation captured in his 1975 book *The Geometry of Meaning*, begins with the twelve measures needed to describe a body's motion, force and power, which can all be matched to signs. Thus acceleration = Aries, mass control = Taurus, and so on up till Pisces, in which case moment of inertia = Pisces. This was before sign effects were disconfirmed, but the explanations do not give precise details about how things like the Moon's opposition to Saturn indicates problems with a person's mother, or the difficulty in correlating physical things to corresponding celestial bodies, when actual planetary positions no longer exist as shown in progressed charts and returns.

(c) <u>Information Theories</u>: The publication notes that since astrologers often say astrology is "non-causal", the switch to information theory seemed a promising one for them. The basic idea of the theory is that information can be treated much like a physical quantity such as energy. But energy is opined as the stuff of causation, while information is weightless and "energyless" and therefore does not imply causation. Besides is there a carrier wave by which information is transmitted? How much information is in the heavens as shown in the birth chart? How quickly can that information be transmitted from the heavens?

(d) Psychic Theories: Many astrologers claim a successful chart reading is dependent on the intuition or psychic ability of the astrologer, and that a birth chart acts like a crystal ball. They see astrology more as something linked to divination, where "its reliability depends on the quality of the astrologers' intuition" (Phillipson 2000:167), implying that the rules, methodologies and instruments are not in themselves the vehicle of interpretation, but rather psychic intuitions and abilities. The problem with this is that psychic abilities aren't scientific and according to findings, careful tests have shown that astrologers do not have useful psychic abilities (Dean & Kelly 2002), nor for that matter do leading psychics (Boerenkamp 1988)[44].

(e) <u>Theories of Magic</u>: It seems that "the most popular explanation of astrology is based on magical correspondences or arguments by analogy, the assumption that things similar in some respects are also similar in other respects. Thus Mars the red planet indicates blood, anger and war, and then by extension anything vaguely red, hot or aggressive". It is not surprising that there is a correlation between this observation and an earlier observation made in the preceding points in this study. An ancient Hermetic writing is quoted to show a sort of affinity shared with astrology: ""The macrocosm has animals, terrestrial and aquatic; in the same way, man has fleas, lice, and tapeworms. The macrocosm has rivers, springs, and seas; man has intestines. The macrocosm contains breaths [winds] springing from its bosom;

[44] Boerenkamp HG (1988). *A Study of Paranormal Impressions of Psychics.* CIP-Gegevens Koninklijke, The Haag. Based on his PhD thesis, University of Utrecht, 1988.

man has flatulence. The macrocosm has Sun and Moon; man has two eyes, the right related to the Sun, the left to the Moon. ... The macrocosm has the twelve signs of the Zodiac; man contains them too, from his head, namely from the Ram, to his feet, which correspond to the Fish" (from MacNiece 1964:126)". A criticism by an astrologer in the person of Dale Huckeby (2003) recognizes that symbolism is too flexible to be useful because it allows an easy accounting of virtually any outcome at any time using any chart, so the match between chart and outcome is non-falsifiable. The old doctrine of correspondences as stated here above has been established to underlie all the so-called occult arts (Hand 1987: p.36).

A careful look at many horoscope sites, regular astrological articles and the general operational space of astrological practitioners today, will reveal strong links to such other mystical practices as Tarot reading, Paranormal and Psychic activities, consultation with Mediums, Crystal-balling, Sorcery and such other mystical practices. Much more, the explanations offered by these practitioners point to the fact that the larger part of the sentiments raised above are still very much imbued in the tenets of astrology even today.

3.2.3 The Test of Natural Empiricism

There really isn't anything directly unscientific about *hypothesizing* the scientificity of astrology; ideas and theories always seem to be welcome in the sciences, but the process of science requires that good questions are asked about any hypothesis under consideration. Some of the important questions for astrology must then be: does the hypothesis of astrology work? Is it supported by observations? Is there any known physical mechanism or established theory by which we can explain astrology? Assuming without conceding that astrological influences truly exist, do these influences work in the way they are said to? Under this sub-heading, we consider some empirical observations that have cast serious doubts on the ability of astrology to make successful predictions, or that the predictions made are at best vague, generalized and therefore of little empirical value. Before proceeding into the evaluation of these tests, some important points are noted from the foregoing on the abstractive nature of astrology. This position on the abstractive character of astrology is deduced from the evaluations that have emerged in this study thus far, and they are that:

(i) The actual size of the constellations differ from one another and therefore it is impossible for the time frames of the apparent transit of the sun in each constellation to be equal. There are wide variations in the amount of days spent in each constellation as opposed to the equal number of days astrology presents, this is surely a major flaw of astrology.

(ii) The sun actually passes through thirteen (13) constellations as recognized even in Ptolemy's works and by the modern Astronomical Union[45]. The bottom part of this thirteenth constellation called "*Ophiuchus*" interjects between Scorpio and Sagittarius, and it is a wonder that this has no bearing on the construct of the Zodiac.

(iii) The constellations are constantly drifting apart because of the precession of the equinoxes. This drift implies that there can be no permanence in their positions.

(iv) By virtue of the precession of the equinoxes, the current physical order of the constellations has radically departed from what it used to be at the time they were adopted by astrologers. This means that while in earlier times, the celestial readings of astrologers were actual interpretations of observed movements of real

---

[45] The International Astronomical Union (IAU) was founded in 1919 to promote and safeguard the science of astronomy in all its aspects, including research, communication, education and development, through international cooperation.

celestial bodies, today all such readings are imaginary, speculative and totally out of touch with reality. This mystifies and trumps the entire construct of astrology.

(v) Despite all these changes mentioned, astrology has remained the same, with the same narratives, same instruments, same methods, and dotted by arbitrary variations in theories and practices, which further compound the problem of its believability.

What an incredible science!

Several years ago some 18 Nobel Laureates and 172 other leading scientists came together to express their vigorous objections to astrology[46] and classified it as a pseudoscience. Also the Committee for the Scientific Investigation of Claims of the Paranormal (CSICOP), once released a statement saying, "Dozens of tests in recent years by scientists can find little, if any, evidence for astrological claims. Horoscopes have been shown under the most rigorous scientific

---

[46] The Humanist, September/October, 1975.

analysis to fail completely in predicting future events"[47].
Several tests have been conducted particularly between the 1970s and 1980s, and so many more carried out from the start of the millennium on the subject of astrology and its empirical relevance to human affairs. According to Manoj Kamoth (2009) by the year 2000, over one hundred publications had appeared in psychology journals and four hundred in astrology journals, equivalent to about 200 man-years of scientific research (with a text size of 470,000 words)[48]. Some of these tests will be referred to here to glean some insight into the challenges astrology faces.

Shawn Carlson carried out one of the most comprehensive tests[49] on astrology. Carlson set out to test the accuracy of astrological natal charts in determining the personality traits of 193 Subjects

---

[47] Paul Recer, "Scientists Find Fault With Astrologers' Use of Stars," The Dallas Morning News, May 9, 1988, p. 6D.
[48] Manoj Kamoth (2009). "Testing Astrology", Current Science, Vol. 96, NO. 12, 25.
[49] Carlson, Shawn (1985). "A Double-blind Test of Astrology". Nature Journal, 318(6045): 419-425.

(aged 17+ yrs). The experiment showed that astrological correctness in matching the extracted data was a matter of chance. Even in situations during the experiments when the astrologers expressed high confidence that they had prognosticated correctly, it didn't make a difference as to the frequency of correctness being by chance. The astrologers in the experiment weren't able to match natal charts to their corresponding personality evaluations better than mere chance, and this "clearly refutes the astrological hypothesis". The experiment was performed in a double-bind manner, with twenty-eight (28) astrologers who had pedigree among their peers and were all vetted by the National Council for Geocosmic Research (NCGR)—all twenty-eight were approved by NCGR, though it nominated twenty-six out (26) of the twenty-eight (28) and approved the remaining two who were interested astrologers and satisfied necessary requirements. The NGCR acted as advisor to the astrologers to ensure fairness and there was a prior agreement before the experiment began by the astrologers agreeing with the experimental protocol as providing a "fair test" for astrology. The astrologers were to match 100 natal charts for psychological profiles provided for the sake of the test. The psychological profiles were provided by the California Psychological Inventory (CPI), to which the astrologers themselves identified as the scientific instrument that was best aligned with the type of information they could divine from their practice. The test showed no correlation.

In Vol. 96, No. 5 of the *Current Science* Journal of 10th March 2009, a paper[50] was published detailing the result of a test conducted by J.V. Narlikar, S. Kunte, N. Dabholkar, and P. Ghatpande to test the potential of "jyortisha" astrology (Indian Astrology) to predict academic ability in people. Two hundred details of students were collected in two groups of hundred each, with one hundred for bright students (Group A) and the other one hundred for mentally retarded students (Group B). The details

[50] "In This Issue". *Current Science,* Vol.96, No. 5, 2009, pp.624. retrieved from
http://www.jstor.org/stable/24104536

were used to cast horoscopes of birth charts for these students, after which the charts were mixed and randomized. Fifty-one astrologers participated in the test and were each given a random set of birth charts, for which they were to use the information provided on the birth charts to interpret the position of the celestial bodies at the birth of each student and thus determine through astrological prediction which of the groups each student would belong to. The statistical analysis of the results showed a failure of the astrologers to prove a measurable level of accuracy and successful matches looked like the product of chance. The same samples were given to an astrological institute for its own analysis, and the institute itself didn't fare any better. The test concluded that astrology doesn't have any predictive power as far as academic ability is concerned.

In another test[51] conducted by Bernie Silverman (1971) to evaluate (a) if astrology yields valid

[51] Bernie Silverman (1971). "Studies of Astrology". **Article** *in* The Journal of Psychology Interdisciplinary and Applied 77(2):141-149 · March 1971. Request copy at https://www.researchgate.net/publication/232543220_Stud

personality descriptions, and (b) why many people feel that it does. The test concluded that traditional astrology is invalid because (a) 1600 undergraduates failed to respond to the Rokeach Value Survey in a manner predicted by astrologers; and (b) patterns of divorce and marriage, personality contingent behaviors, did not correspond to astrological predictions. Bernie Silverman surveyed astrologers across the country on the compatibility of the twelve Zodiac signs. In studying, 2,978 marriages and 478 divorce records in Michigan, Silverman found couples whose marriages by horoscope traditions ought to last longer due to personality compatibility, also united and split up with the same frequency as those who were not astrologically compatible. The study also concluded that the variable of membership group saliency seemed to contribute to astrology's followership, because only when astrological descriptions were labeled as such did persons

---

ies_of_Astrology . (PsycINFO Database Record (c) 2012 APA).

correlate the descriptions as being an accurate portrait of themselves.

Hartmanna .P., Reuterb .M., and Nyborga .H. (2005) of the Individual Differences Research Unit (IDRU), University of Aarhus, Department of Psychology, Denmark, investigated[52] the relationship between date of birth and individual differences in personality and intelligence. Using over fifteen thousand (15,000+) samples from two separate collections; the first being a sample of over four thousand (4,000+) middle-aged males from the Vietnam Experience Study; while the second consisted of over eleven thousand (11,000+) young adults from the data gathered from the National Longitudinal Study of Youth carried out in 1979 and extracted from ten subsets of the Armed Services Vocational Aptitude Battery. The test also sought to

[52] Hartmanna .P., Reuterb .M., and Nyborga .H. (2005). "The Relationship between Date of Birth and Individual Differences in Personality and General Intelligence: A Large-scale Study". © 2005 Elsevier Ltd. Published online by *Personality and Individual Differences* 40 (2006) 1349–1362.

test Eysenck's notion of possible relationships between date of birth and the popular sun signs in astrology. The study concluded that in none of the cases did date of birth relate to individual differences in personality or general intelligence, and that no support could be found for possible relationships between dates of births and popular sun signs in astrology.

In a 1977 experiment[53], physicist John McGervey of Case Western Reserve University Ohio cross-checked the birthdays of 16,634 scientists listed in "American Men of Science" and 6,475 politicians named in "Who's Who in American Politics". Astrological theory by its design would suggest that these two classes of Americans would fall among specific zodiac signs and personality types due to their occupations; however McGervey found the groups had about the same number of people born under each sign of the zodiac, so that there were as many Virgos—who in astrological m terms are

---

[53] McGervey J.D. (1977). "A Statistical Test of Sun-Sign Astrology". *The Zetec,* Vol. 1, No. 2, p.53.

defined as weak leaders—as any other sign. The test concluded that there was no support for the astrological theory.

In a 2003 publication[54], G. Dean and I.W. Kelly reported their studies on time twins, i.e. subjects of the experiment who were born within minutes of each other and shared the same sun sign. The discovery was that if they were raised differently, their characters turned out to be individually different. The study evaluated 2,000 people who were born within minutes of each other, tracked them for several decades, and deeply considered over a hundred (100) different characteristics, ranging from occupation to sports, sociability levels, IQ, anxiety, and ability in art. All these are traits which astrology claims are influenced by heavenly bodies, but the test found no similarities in the predictive typologies of the personalities or other character similarities that astrology claims to foretell.

---

[54] Geoffrey Dean and Ivan .W. Kelly (2003). "Is Astrology Relevant to Consciousness and Psi?" *Journal of Consciousness Studies,* Vol. 10, pp. 6-7. Search at www.imprint.co.uk/jcs.html

Dean Geoffrey (2015) in a combined review[55] of three studies, to test the effects of sun signs on compatibility in love and married couples, observes that the recent studies (Sachs 1998[56], Castille 2004[57], Voas 2007[58]) with a combined sample size of 27 million couples—a combination of the largest known sample size—failed to find the slightest evidence for sun sign effects for couples. In response to possible astrologers' claim that sun signs alone do not determine accurate predictions, Voas (2007) argues that astrology has influenced everyday belief almost entirely through the use of sun signs; if sun signs are then seen as useless when it comes to assessing

[55] Dean Geoffrey, (2015). "Love Signs Fail World's Largest Tests (N=27m)". Available at http://www.astrology-and-science.com/S-love2.htm
[56] Gunter Sachs (1998). "The Astrology File". Published in paperback by Orion, London (1999).
[57] Didier Castille, (2004). "Birth Day Effect on Natality Rhythms". *Correlation* 22.2, 20-32.
[58] David Voas, (2007). "Ten Million Marriages: A Test of Astrological 'Love Signs' ". Carthie Marsh Centre for Census and Survey research, University of Manchester.

personality and romantic compatibility, then astrology would lose its hold on the public imagination.

There have also been several other studies carried out by astrologers themselves to prove the regularity, relevance and credibility in astrological predictions, some of these tests had positive correlations with astrological claims, but have largely been difficult to replicate. Starting from the very famous research efforts of French psychologist Michel Gauquelin, who conducted a statistical test[59] of personalities of people born under various signs of the zodiac to verify if there is a correlation between traits indicated in Zodiac signs and actual personality traits. In this particular study, he listed 50,000 character traits of 16,000 famous people. Gauquelin then assigned the appropriate zodiac sign to each trait such as Leo, Aries, Pisces etc. He found no correlation between personality traits and the sign a person was born under.

---

[59] Nigel Henbest (1987). "Misreading the Stars," Word Press Review, September, p. 55.

However, Gauquelin is also known to have found some sort of correlations between the occupations of athletes with when Mars occupies a certain position in the sky. This has been widely known as the "Mars Effect"[60] and has sparked more studies in the same direction, but attempts by other researchers to replicate this Gauquelin study has been met with inconsistent results. Also, the "sectors" that the sky is divided into which Gauquelin relied on to get his results are not related to the traditional divisions by astrology of the sky, which makes Gauquelin's study more of an evidence against the method that astrologers use. In a response to Eysenck's[61] evaluation of the Mars Effect, Prof Marcello Truzzi[62] states that "the case for neo-

---

[60] Guaquelin Michel (1988). "Is There Really a Mars Effect?". *Above & Below: Journal of Astrological Studies,* Issue 11, pp. 4-7.

[61] Hans Jürgen Eysenck, was a German-born English psychologist who tried to expand on Guaquelin's work and is himself popular for studies on intelligence and personality.

[62] Marcello Truzzi (1984) "A Response to Eysenck's Evaluation of the Mars Effect". *Journal of Astro-Psychological Problems*, 2.2, 27

astrological causalities being present in Gauquelins' work is greatly strengthened" by consideration of the total corpus of their researches. And this context increases the scientific importance and priority their work should be accorded, while also adding to the over-all extraordinariness of their anomalies. On the other hand, the Gauquelin and Eysenck work (though presenting…real and important anomalies) still represents an extraordinary set of claims for which commensurate proof has not yet been obtained".

3.3 ARGUMENTS FOR AND AGAINST

Much of the arguments and empirical analyses that have been presented so far in this study have scrutinized the scientific claims of astrology, pointing out how there isn't sufficient data to concretize its claims despite the avalanche of studies that have been carried out; and that the innate character of its theories aren't consistent with known methods of science. But at this point, some major arguments cited by those in defense of astrology will be considered so as to have a look at the perspectives from which astrologers view the contexts of the problems raised by critics.

Teri Gee (2012) in a study[63] identifies certain defenses for astrology. He reminds us of the philosophical principle of determinism and its relationship with astrology—inherent in this philosophy is the idea that all events and phenomena have a necessary cause (i.e. all things have a cause) which determines their occurrence. Astrology claims that essentially, social phenomena in human affairs are caused, albeit under the causative influence of the stars. Determinism on its own was a subject of some controversy in ancient philosophy, sparking several debates. According to the Stoics, *"There is nothing outside the cosmos and thus there is nothing external which can affect it. Within the cosmos every individual part, from the stars to plants to people, is connected through a network of causes which affects every aspect of the cosmos. They cannot be avoided*

---

[63] Teri Gee (2012). *"Strategies of Defending Astrology: A Continuing Tradition"*. Institute for the History and Philosophy of Science and Technology, University of Toronto.

because there is no way of removing oneself from the network of causes. That would require removing oneself from the universe". Strict determinism is one which eliminates man's free will and says everything is determined or fated; while limited determinism preserves the human free will but still acknowledges the stars as causes, even as primary causes in the sublunar realm. However, Teri Gee acknowledges that this does not automatically give rise to an ability to predict the exact courses of events. Although there is a cause for every event, these causes are not strictly linear; rather, "there is an eternal causal nexus, where cause gives rise to cause,"[64] meaning that we may not be able to see what has caused every event to take place, but all events are caused. Teri Gee further considered four critics of astrology in antiquity and presents counter-arguments against them, to wit:

> **(i)   Cicero's   Argument:** The summary of Cicero's argument

---

[64] Frede, Dorothea, (2003). "Stoic Determinism," in B. Inwood (ed) *Cambridge Companion to the Stoics*. Cambridge: CUP, pp. 179-205.

could be put in his own words *"For we do not apply the words 'chance,' 'luck,' 'accident,' or 'casualty' except to an event which has so occurred or happened that it either might not have occurred at all, or might have occurred in any other way. How, then, is it possible to foresee and to predict an event that happens at random, as the result of blind accident, or of unstable chance?"* He further says that "Then what becomes of that vaunted divination of you Stoics? For if all things happen by Fate, it does us no good to be warned to be on our guard, since that which is to happen will happen regardless of what we do." He buttresses this point by referring to the lives of twins, focusing on the fact that they are born at almost identical

154

times, thus under the same arrangement of the heavens but often have very different lives.

(ii) **<u>Favorinus' Argument:</u>** Favorinus was a Sophist and his arguments were similar to those of Cicero, he is said to have referred to astrology as a practice of *"tricks and delusions"* which have been *"devised by jugglers and men who made a living and profit from their lies"*. According to Gee (2009), Favorinus argues that even if it could actually be true, no man lives long enough to understand all the details of the movements of the heavens and the stars are so far away that it is impossible that anyone could actually predict the future using a knowledge of their movements. Illustrations on the problem of twins having the same astrological signs but different lives, including the difficulty of similar predictions for large numbers of people, mass deaths, and the usefulness of foretelling the future as it relates to human emotions, are some of the points upon which Favorinus elaborated on his rejection of astrology.

(iii)   **Sextus Empiricus' Argument:** Being a Skeptic, Sextus Empiricus argued against the possibility of knowing anything at all. He contends that astrologers build *"a great bulwark of superstition against us"* and allow *"us to do nothing according to right reason"*. Favorinus believed that astrology's effectiveness hung on its ties to destiny because if fate did not cause every event in every life, then astrology could not exist.

He further poses that *"If he who was born in the pitcher of Aquarius is doomed to suffer shipwreck, how is it that the Greeks who were being brought back from Troy were all drowned together round the 'Hollows' of Euboea?"* They all could not have been born in the pitcher of Aquarius, and if they were not, and it was only one man who was destined to die in a shipwreck, *"what reason is there why this man's destiny overmasters the destinies of them all, rather than that they should all be saved because of one man whose destiny it is to die on dry land?"*

(iv) **Plotinus' Argument:** Is credited by Gee (2009) to have given a more rounded critique compared to the earlier three. Being a third-century Neoplatonist, Gee identifies two elements in the arguments of Plotinus that baffle him (i.e. Plotinus) on the claims of astrology and they are:

- Preserving human free will and explaining how human beings can have autonomy if all their actions are dictated by the movements and arrangements of the stars; and

- Maintaining the divinity of the stars. If the stars cause events in the sublunary world, then they cause both good and evil events, meaning that something divine is the source of evil which cannot happen.

According to Gee, Plotinus was willing to look at other variants beyond the all-or-nothing debates around astrology—i.e. arguments that the stars cause every action in the sublunary realm—

which pervaded his day. He rather seemed to align with an astrology in which the stars are signs of the future but not causes. Though Plotinus states that all things have a physical cause of some sort and thus celestial bodies are wont to, but he contends against the supposition that all things are caused by the celestial, and posits that the so-called causal influence of the celestial realm cannot take away freewill. He also insists that the stars cannot directly cause evil acts.

One common thread we see in Gee's review of astrology shows that the questions have been the same, only that they have taken different dimensions in different civilizations. All four scholars at some point referred to a lack of physical mechanism, empirical inconsistencies, and the speculative nature of astrology. We then see a modification by Plotinus who concedes to the possibility of the stars signposting possible events of the future so as to allow people make a more informed decision and use their freewill to alter the course of their lives in the direction they desire. This is limited determinism, which states that all things are caused, but freewill plays a role. This argument is a reproduction of a previous argument by astrologers mentioned elsewhere in this text, which emphasizes the role of astrology as a preparatory forecast, showing possible future courses which can be used to guide human decisions. Though the question of this relevance in empirical terms hasn't been settled. Ptolemy provided the first rational explanation devoid of influences of the gods, and his defense centered around the definition of astrology (he admits that one necessarily "ascribes to it the weakness and predictability of material qualities [i.e. the sublunar world]" because it isn't as exact as its counterpart which is explainable by mathematics, but must accept that astrology is possible because "it is so evident that most events of a general nature draw their causes from the enveloping heavens."); the relevance of astrology (because if the celestial objects have obvious general effects, "why not particular effects as well?...For the sun, together with the ambient, is always in some way affecting everything on the earth," such as the changing temperature, the passing seasons and even the breeding of animals. In addition, the moon, "as the heavenly body nearest the earth, bestows her effluence..." most particularly on the waters, based on the various phases. And so by more knowledge, he believes the inexact variables in astrology could be resolved, since the deficiency is actually that of human knowledge). The benefits of astrology *(which is in the foreknowledge that it provides and the appropriation which society can make of such "forecast" would help in perceiving what is fitting and expedient for the capabilities of each temperament of persons)* is on the grounds of the context of determinism as a positive outflow of astrology. *"For, in the first place, we should consider that even with events that will necessarily take place, their unexpectedness is very apt to cause excessive pain and delirious joy, while foreknowledge accustoms and calms the soul by experience of distant events as though they were present and prepares it to greet with calm and steadiness whatever comes."*

161

A careful assessment of the defenses provided by Ptolemy will reveal a continuing tradition today, save that they are in more sophisticated contexts and in a more competitive environment. First is the issue that if the sun and moon have such effects on our climatic conditions, why should we rule out their influence in other areas? While accommodating this thought, it is important to note that the actual contention is in creating an empirical link to the influence of celestial objects on terrestrial life. Also, the value that astrologers seek to project with their arguments in the defense of astrology should not be shoved aside carelessly, like Ptolemy, they argue that much of the antagonism to astrology is largely due to ignorance of what it actually means and ignorance of all the factors that need to come together in interpreting the diverse pieces of information to make an accurate prognosis or forecast. This may be true and shouldn't be a basis to discriminate against it as an academic field, but in the same vein, astrology must realize that much of the criticisms it has faced isn't peculiar to it, as even such a prestigious subject as Economics, which is regarded as a cornerstone social science has itself been faced with these vagaries. Hence, if astrology will improve its lot through its desire to acquire scientific status, its craft must reach the minimum bar, or simply just remain as a unique art until it can do so.

The benefits that astrologers claim to offer are in themselves questionable. Though admittedly in the chaos of today's global economy, people are more desperate for hope and are in need of ways to interpret the uncertainties of life in order to retain their sanity, the dangers however that the disparities in the forecasts portend are even more harmful if society leans on the generalized postures of these statements which are in sharp conflict with observable data. False hopes, misinformation, baseless assumptions and sheer falsehood have a potential to cause more strains on the emotional ecosystem, with severe adverse consequences. The efforts of scholarly research and criticism is to help society appreciate the current empirical realities as against the claims of astrology.

Dr. Soundar Divakar in his evaluation[65] contends on some of the misconstructions and misunderstandings that characterize much of the critique on astrology. Though giving his insight from the perspective of Indian astrology, he raises some interesting posers that are useful in the broad context of astrology. His reference to Percy Seymour's prognostications in an offered defense of the astrological theory—a theory which had at the time come under severe bashings in the West—offers invaluable insights. Here are some of Davikar's arguments:

1. That, in a large number of horoscopes of parents and their children, some interesting similarities can be found. A few planets, not necessarily Jupiter and Saturn (which according to him take 11.8613 and 29.4568 years to complete one revolution around the sun, and hence can easily justify repeatability), are in either similar positions or

[65] Divakar, Soundar. (2009). "The Science of Astrology". *The Astrological Magazine*, Vol. 98. Pp. 21-22.

in similar combinations in the horoscopes of parents and their children. This to him cannot be a coincidence. If the planets do not have a genetic correlation, this above 'inheritance' will not occur. He argues that the legendary French Astrologer, Michel Gauquelin had proved this point to the amazement of strong critics who could not ignore this particular point of inheritance in their analyses of Gauquelin's data. Divakar (2009) believes this is one of the strongest points which proves the relationship between genetics and Astrology.

2. That Percy Seymour in his book[66] posits a **Scientific Theory** that related planetary influences to human beings. According to him, Seymour (1990) had proposed that due to the varying gravitational influence of planets on the magnetic field of the Sun, the magnetic

---

[66] P. A. H. Seymour, (1990). *"Astrology: The Evidence of Science"* (Revised and extended paperback version), Great Britain: Arkana-Penguin.

perturbations created in the sun, each being specific to individual planets, produce variations in the Solar Wind, which when it reaches the earth, continuously affects the fetus at the time of its birth. The influence of each planet in tune with the already expressed (formed) genetic characteristics, influences the child at birth and keeps influencing it when it grows. Each individual planet is described as being able to play a selective role in influencing human beings because the **Sun** amplifies the gravitational effects of the planets in the form of magnetic field variation, which is transmitted to the earth, thereby affecting human beings. Divakar asserts that even today, prominent critics on Astrology are finding it difficult to denounce this explanation.

3. That the Rahu - Ketu axis, representing the two intersecting points in the orbital plane of the Earth (Ecliptic) to that of the Moon, are also considered important so much so that

they are treated as two planets; and that the planets between Ketu - Rahu axis do have different connotations in astrology that are well known for their importance in health, wealth, intelligence, relations, family, wife/husband, friends, longevity, diseases, honour, profession, luck and even losses! According to Divakar, if astrology is not a science, why should two points in space connected with the orbital plane of the earth assume so much significance?

4. That it is now unequivocally established in the sciences that characteristics of individuals are attributable to their genes, such that visible characteristics like appearance, speech, intellect and diseases, to name a few, are related to the genes. He argues that the fact that planetary combinations can be used to describe them is another clear indication that planetary influences play a decisive role in controlling genetic expressions in individuals.

5. That the **Unifield Field Theory** and its related **String (and recently Brane) Theory** are still contemplating on 10-32 dimensional (or more) universe with four dimensions of space and time and the remaining probably hidden dimensions. Astrology clearly describes the multi-dimensional characteristics of the universe. To his mind, Divakar believes that Astrology links huge masses like planets on the one hand to humans who are characterized by genes made up of strands of DNA molecules. In this way, it represents unification of all the four fundamental forces (i.e. electromagnetic, strong nuclear , weak nuclear and gravitational) whereas science is still unable to bring all these four fundamental forces together, because gravity defies unification while the other three forces-strong , weak and electromagnetic forces-have been successfully integrated.

In considering these highlighted arguments from the others in his publication, it is doubtful if these theoretical claims have been proven. For it to be theoretical enough, there must be sufficient data and empirical analysis to back the claims of theoretical possibilities. There is no doubt that Seymour improves on the explanatory power of the possible links of astrological/planetary influences, but much of his analysis is largely based on the possibility of "multi-link theories" and a disapproval of what Seymour considers a dogmatic bigotry of the critics of astrology. Seymour says that *"from the viewpoint of the philosophy of science, any number of theories may be shown not to work, but to say it follows that no theory of astrology can work is just bad science. It totally rules out scientific method. So, having examined the arguments that supposedly disproved astrology, I came to the conclusion that they were totally unscientific - a form of rationalized bigotry cloaked in academic language"* (see Dr. Percy Seymour's interview at http://cura.free.fr/decem/09seym.html[67]).

---

[67]"The Magus of Magnetism" (An Interview with Dr. Percy Seymour) **by Bronwyn Elko.** *This interview first*

Divakar himself doesn't embark on any direct empirical tests, and much of his references have either been controverted for heavy bias, as in the Gauquelin case, or do not adduce any physical evidence of observed data to prove any hypothesis. For instance Dr. Seymour's remark that *"What I think might be happening is that the fetus's neural network acts as a sort of antenna that tunes into fluctuations in Earth's magnetic field"*, shows that his explanations are still speculative and do not yet have any empirical validity yet, talk more of establishing a theoretical foundation. Though at the time of the interview, Dr. Seymour did indicate that there was on-going work by him and his students on the possible results of a thesis on planetary dominance in the solar cycle, which may provide a fundamental underpinning for astrology, but it is not certain that the outcomes of his study put paid to the issues raised. The text *"A New Theory for the Solar Cycle"*

appeared in **The Mountain Astrologer (Issue #80, Aug./Sept. 1998)** and is available at: http://cura.free.fr/decem/09seym.html .Retrieved 13th March 2019.

by P.A.H. Seymour and M.J. Willimott had its explanations solely based on a calculative analysis of certain principles of physics and mathematics that might apply to the new theoretical propositions, but they were all this theoretical speculations without any subsequent back up by data. This could be a significantly important area for further research on the subject.

3.4 UNANSWERED QUESTIONS

Some of the unanswered questions in view of scientific enquiry and measures to determine the reliability of astrology are harvested below as a focal reminder of the facts in issue.

The University of California Museum of Paleontology, Berkeley, and the Regents of the University of California in a 2008 checklist[68] identified some factors that should be used in measuring whether or not astrology is a science. This

---

checklist presented is a good way to formulate some good questions on the subject.

How scientific is Astrology?

1. ☐ **Does it focus on the natural world?**

2. ☐ **Does it aim to explain the natural world?**

3. ☐ **Does it use testable ideas?**

4. ☐ **Does it rely on evidence?**

5. ☐ **Does it involve the scientific community?**

6. ☐ **Does it lead to ongoing research?**

7. ☐ **Do the researchers behave**

   scientifically?

Astrology could be said to focus on the planetary arrangements and how the movements of these celestial bodies affect personal, group or universal human affairs in the terrestrial. In this sense it could be said to focus on the natural world, particularly if we choose to look away from the mystical origins associated with the planetary motions and their mythical symbolisms. It could also be said to aim to explain the natural world, e.g. why does Mr. A act the way he does? And why does Mr. B act differently? These questions are relevant to personality types. The difficult questions are whether it uses testable ideas, whether it relies on evidence, whether it involves the scientific community, if it leads to ongoing research or whether the researchers in its field behave scientifically. Question numbers three through seven, seem to be where astrology is lax. Not that the ideas are not testable at all, such a view would be dogmatic, but the tests largely do not validate the astrological predictions. Apart from the divergence between empirical observations and astrological claims, the science community's involvement in verification and validity endeavors have largely not been by the astrologers themselves, they more like wait for others to validate or contradict their ideas, which is a negation of scientific behavior. Add these to the static nature of astrology in its contribution to research over the years and you begin to see why most scientists are wary of astrology as a subject.

Other questions that could be asked include:

• Can the ideas of astrology be used to make predictions about what will happen under particular circumstances or at a specific time in the future?—this touches on repeatability of tests.

• Have the predictions been tested?

• What evidence is required to prove the idea wrong?

• Do conclusions in this area undergo peer review in a mainstream scientific journal?

These are questions that astrology hasn't been able to satisfactorily answer in the positive. Accordingly, a proper explanation of astrology should reveal how the planets, the sun, the moon, and other celestial bodies can correspond to people, thus allowing the derivation of intelligible astrological principles. It should provide sufficient insights to questions such as[69]: how does astrology really work?

---

[69] *"Theories of Astrology: A comprehensive survey"*. Retrieved from www.astrology-and-science.com/a-theo2.htm on 10th April 2019.

Why are there disparities between empirical data and astrological claims? Why is the time of birth preferable to the time of conception? How does astrology predict events and answer queries? Will signs be relevant if they are not attached to celestial objects? Why are the adopted ecliptic positions preferred to the real positions? What techniques are most suited to particular situations? What should a chart contain and why? What role does the personality of the astrologer play in the consultation process? These and more are pressing voids that astrology needs to fill if it will be taken seriously within the sciences, as of now it falls short of a science and should not be regarded as such.

CHAPTER FOUR
ASTROLOGY AS A PSUEDOSCIENCE

In this study, we have seen that the term pseudoscience refers to a body of false or extremely improbable ideas that might sound scientific but do not have supporting evidence and are in conflict with scientific consensus. There are certain attributes that characterize a pseudoscience, and they include:

1. Use of vague, exaggerated or unstable claims that have no clear explanatory power and often require additional unsupported assumptions. Pseudoscientific claims do not properly articulate, if at all they do, well-defined limitations under which their predictions apply or do not apply[70].

2. Excessive reliance on affirmation rather than rebuttals. Adherents give no room for the possibility that their assertions could be wrong, and seek to suppress data that invalidate their claims while amplifying the slightest data that are supportive. This is contrary to the scientific method[71].

---

[70] Hines Terrence (1988). *"Pseudoscience and the Paranormal: A Critical Examination of the Evidence"*. Buffalo, NY: Prometheus Books. *ISBN 978-0-87975-419-8*.
[71] Lakatos I (1970). *"Falsification and the Methodology of*

3. Evasion of peer review before publishing results and a lack of receptivity to probation by other experts[72]. There is a secretive disposition to data and a tendency to personalize contentions around debates and theory validation.

4. Failure to provide progressive evidence of its theoretical claims[73]. A pseudoscience is not self-correcting despite new evidence, does not improve in its theorization, neither does it add more explanations or evidence to its foundational claims.

5. Use of suppositious language that sound scientific. These words are used in a manner that they acquire a special meaning apart from the normal scientific meaning. This creates an impression of organized scientific knowledge,

Scientific Research Programmes". In Lakatos I, Musgrave A. Criticism and the Growth of Knowledge. pp. 91–195.
[72] Hines, Ibid.
[73]Paul R. Thagard, (1978) "Why Astrology Is A Pseudoscience". Philosophy of Science Association Journal, Vol. 1, pp. 223-234.

whereas the theoretical basis isn't scientific in nature neither is it validated by evidence.

4.1 ASTROLOGY AND ITS BELIEF SYSTEM

Astrology in ancient times was closely related to astronomy, meteorology, medicine and alchemy. Its chief belief is that the positioning of celestial objects has a huge influence on human affairs. It also believes that human affairs are not only influenced by the planets, but also by what is called the collective unconscious, in which the present reality is experienced and information is divined through the interpretation of omens. Western Astrology is dependent on charts and the skills of the astrologer, the use of horoscopes which explain traits of personalities, and the prediction of future events based on the sun, moon, planetary positions, and symbolisms of the zodiac (i.e. divisions of the ecliptic into 12 constellations). Other things such as the Four Elements, Aspects, Houses, Ascendant and date of birth play different roles. Along with Tarot reading, it is one of the core studies of western Esotericism, and has influenced Hermeticism and such systems as Wicca. After its decline from the academic circles in the 17th century due to theoretical advancements, it bore little significance in academic and social discourse until the general revival of spiritualism in 19th century and the advent of the New Age Philosophy[74].

4.2 MYSTICISM, SPIRITISM, CHIROMANCY AND ASTROLOGY

The American colonies and subsequently the United States have been described to have been a home to esoteric practitioners of alchemy, astrology, mysticism and magic until they waned under the waxing influence of rationalist philosophy, science and industrialism[75]. Folk magic traditions in America were closely related with a synthesis of astrology, magic, herbalism, and religious practices handed

---

[74] https://www.crystalinks.com/astrology.html
[75] Arthur Versluis. *Magic and Mysticism: An Introduction to Western Esotericism.* Rowman and Littlefield, P.140.

down trans-generationally. Titus Burkhardt in his review[76] of the works on mystical astrology by the great Islamic scholar Muhyiddin Ibn' Arabi, in which Arabi encloses the facts of hermetic astrology in the edifice of his cosmology, and shows that in its entirety this effort could point to metaphysical principles relating to a knowledge that is self-sufficient in itself. In his work, there seems to be a distillation of spiritual astrology from divinatory astrology, but strong ties are made to Plato's cosmology which argues the permeation of all materiality by the divine presence. Arabi however situates this idea of Plato within the Islamic worldview and ascribes the same divine permeation and reference to such factors as the *"orientation of the spirit"*. Titus observes that *"correspondences with the three worlds or degrees of human existence, such as appear in the symbolism of the angelic functions to which are related the twelve zodiacal*

---

[76] Titus Burckhardt, "Mystical Astrology According to Ibn 'Arabi ". Beshara Publications, Abingdon, England (1977).

signs…should be understood starting with the reflections of the intellectual terrain in the nature of the cycle, and according to the perspective of the production of these three worlds".

These thoughts clearly link astrology with mystical, spiritual and spiritist heritages which are by their nature not verifiable under scientific instruments, though they are mixed with other aspects of observable phenomena. On the other hand, Chiromancy, according to an astrology site[77], "is another form of divination, where markings on the palm of the hand (as well as the shape of the hand, length of the fingers, and more) are used to tell a person about their life, and what is likely to happen". So chiromancy also makes predictions, but instead it takes its readings from the palm instead of the skies and asserts its claims with no natural explanations. This is very similar to the mannerisms of astrology, and on the field of practice many Astrologers and

---

[77]"Chiromancy". Available at www.astrologyanswers.com/astrology_definitions/c/chiromancy/

Chiromancers share actual vocational affiliations. So it is easier to see why astrology largely assumes a posture of inerrant knowledge even when such knowledge is contradicted by observable facts, because the gods, the spiritual plane, or the supreme divinity from where the knowledge comes cannot be wrong.

4.3 ARTISTIC IMPRECISION AND "SCIENTIFICATION" (Vagueness generalistic)

According to *The American Heritage Dictionary of the English Language,* mysticism is:

"A spiritual discipline aiming at union with the divine through deep meditation or trancelike contemplation…Any belief in the existence of realities beyond perceptual or intellectual apprehension but central to being and directly accessible by intuition."

Mystical arts claim union with the divine and with absolute influences which have unique interpretative contexts, intuitive insights and enlightenment. The attempt here is not in any way pejorative, but it aims to highlight why mysticism and science should be classified as separate worlds with separate characteristics and allowed to each attain their relevance within the ambits of their unique intents and the challenges that they each face therefrom. Douglas W. Shrader (2008) identified seven unique characteristics of mystical experiences[78] and they are:

1. Ineffability (i.e. inability to capture the experience in ordinary language);

2. Noetic quality (i.e. the notion that mystical experiences reveal an otherwise hidden or generally inaccessible knowledge);

3. Transciency (i.e. the understanding that mystical experiences last for a relatively brief period of time);

---

[78] Douglas W. Shrader (2007). "*Seven Characteristics of Mystical Experiences*". Presented at the 6th Annual Hawaii International Conference on Arts and Humanities, Honolulu, HI, (2008). Retrieved at http://citeseerx.ist.psu.edu/viewdoc/download?doi=10.1.1.601.4094&rep=rep1&type=pdf

4. Passivity (i.e. the inclination that mystical experiences are somehow beyond the control of human volition);

5. Unity of opposites (i.e. a sense of Oneness, Wholeness or Completeness);

6. Timelessness (i.e. a perception that mystical experiences transcend time);

7. Encounter with the "True self" (i.e. a kind of awareness of one's true cosmic self beyond life and death, difference and duality, and ego and selfishness).

Going by Shrader's observations, which largely agrees with other supportive canvasses of mystic experiences; ineffability likely explains the gaps in explanatory power; the noetic character explains the airs of exclusivity and inerrancy that characterizes mystical ventures; transciency could be a pointer to the 'off and on' character of intuitive accuracies/inaccuracies; passivity might explain the deterministic ingredients; timelessness may explain why the principles don't change because they bear an eternal aura; while the unity of opposites and "True self" encounters might explain the inherent satisfaction, fulfilment and self-contentment (and in the case of astrology 'self-containment') that mystical artistes exude.

But if astrology hopes to transmogrify from its mystic tendencies into a proper science, then it must be willing to go through a process of "scientification". In the context of this text, "scientification" connotes a submission or adaptation to the thoroughness of the scientific method which we have at different points in this text elaborated on.

4.4 HOROSCOPE/ASTROLOGY AS A TYPE OF PSEUDOSCIENCE

Scholars have varying opinions in the demarcation of science and pseudoscience. As we can deduce from the opening statements of this chapter, many definitions have been presented in defining pseudoscience; another one of them is that a pseudoscience is a failed version of science that does not meet scientific criteria (Stanford Encyclopedia). A close look at a pseudoscience reveals that it leans toward "practical" knowledge instead of scientifically proven facts. In the medieval ages, astrology was widely accepted in many lands and it was taught in Universities as a discipline. The discipline required a working knowledge of certain languages as well as mathematics and was closely linked to science with many theories associated with it. Generally, astrologers were viewed as reputable scholars, as much literature from that period indicates how astrologers really influenced human affairs. For instance, astrologer William Lilly was influential in England in 1600s, and he did advise Parliament in matters of war (Kelly Debra, 2016)[79]. Influential people in society consulted astrologers on various

---

[79] Kelly, Debra (2016). "10 Influential Astrologers that Shaped History." *List Verse*.
https://listverse.com/2016/10/11/10-influential-astrologers-that-shaped-history/.

occasions. They did so before undertaking any project whether it was about traveling, war, construction, or business, astrologers had to be consulted.

Researchers and scholars decided to carry out research to prove whether astrology was a science. Their studies showed that the planets and stars emitted no force that could affect humans the way astrologers claimed. Extensive works of astronomers discredited astrology as a legitimate science. In the seventeenth century, a significant shift in how astrology was perceived began to take shape; and even though most astronomers initially believed in astrology, they well understood how unstable astrology was. Its character as a pseudoscience is manifest in many of its attributes.

Today, astrological calculations are made according to the ancient geocentric view of the planets revolve around the earth, though some astrologers claim that this has nothing to do with the earth being the center of the universe, however with a similar horoscope and from the same geocentric perspective, two astrologers are likely to differ in their findings. Astrological predictions from different astrologers for the same individual often do not match. When astrologers decide to write, their work is not peer-reviewed, unlike scientific articles and journals. There are no documented studies of astrology that contribute to new scientific discovery. Astrological predictions also prove to be too generalized and could apply to anyone.

To consider a final example, astrologers are said to have expressed belief that since weather came from heaven, then it would be logical to believe that the heavens controlled the weather. To prove that fact, some scholars decided to keep accurate records with details of weather patterns. They recorded the weather daily along with the day's horoscope in a bid to determine whether the heavens controlled the weather. They were keen to notice whether any regular patterns would give credibility to astrology. They failed to find any consistent pattern thus further discrediting the idea that astrology is a science. There is just so much empirical odds stacked against the claims of horoscopes and astrology in general.

CHAPTER FIVE

CONCLUSION

The study concludes that astrology originated as man's search for meaning in the sky and its effect on the terrestrial. Early astrologers looked to the sky to interpret weather and seasonal changes, but sooner stretched these validated observations and the scope of their relevance to personal, interpersonal (relationships), group and universal human affairs. Astrology became a culturally transmitted heuristics to explain complexities in human affairs especially as they related to events that mainstream science had obscure explanations for, and in this sense held an appreciable relevance until major theoretical and empirical breakthroughs began to weaken the fabric of its explanatory power. The precession of the equinoxes and the inevitable change in the zodiacal constellations that it implies, coupled with the successful refutation of the geocentric worldview and the discovery that the sun actually transits in its apparent movement through thirteen constellations are pointers to the inherent inconsistencies of astrology. The litany of unanswered questions, use of the Barnum Effect, theoretical posture of inerrancy, stagnation in progressive ideas, severally failed tests at validation, attachment to its mythological and mystic past, and its incompatibility with the scientific method are the solid factors that come together to make it a failed science.

Astrology has been stagnant in its explanatory power, and its cling to a few supporting data in the face of several empirical contradictions do not avail its theories. The reference by Divakar (2009) to Percy Sermour's theoretical prognostications on "multi-link theories" have not gotten sufficient root in empirical analysis and so cannot be adopted as an advancement of its explanatory efforts. Also, the disposition of astrologers to cede the proof of theoretical validity or otherwise of astrology to the efforts of others compounds its position as a pseudoscience.

REFERENCES

1. Adel, M.M.; Hossain, S.F.; and Johnson .H. (2013). "Favored Zodiac for Celebrity Births", Journal of Social Sciences Vol. 9 (4).

2. Amanda Hess (2019). *"How Astrology Took Over The Internet"*, retrieved at https://www.nytimes.com/2018/01/01/arts/how-astrology-took-over-the-internet.html.

3. Andrew Fraknoi (2012) "An Astronomer Looks at Astrology". The Universe at Your Fingertips. Astronomical Society of the Pacific.

4. Arthur Versluis. "*Magic and Mysticism: An Introduction to Western Esotericism".* Rowman and Littlefield, P.140.

5. Bernie Silverman (1971). "Studies of Astrology". **Article** *in* The Journal of Psychology Interdisciplinary and Applied 77(2):141-149 · March 1971. Request copy at https://www.researchgate.net/publication/2325

43220_Studies_of_Astrology . (PsycINFO Database Record (c) 2012 APA).

6. Boerenkamp HG (1988). *A Study of Paranormal Impressions of Psychics.* CIP-Gegevens Koninklijke, The Haag. Based on his PhD thesis, University of Utrecht, 1988.

7. British Library, *"Learning Bodies of Knowledge: Medieval Astrology".* Available at https://web.archive.org/web/20130305064820/ http://www.bl.uk/learning/artimages/bodies/as trology/astrologyhome.html

8. Brown Elko (1998). "The Magus of Magnetism" (An Interview with Dr. Percy Seymour)**.** *This interview first appeared in* **The Mountain Astrologer (Issue #80, Aug./Sept. 1998)** and is available at: http://cura.free.fr/decem/09seym.html .Retrieved 13th March 2019.

9. Carlson, Shawn (1985). "A Double-blind Test of Astrology". *Nature Journal,* 318(6045): 419-425.

10. Campion, Nicholas (2008), *"A History of Western Astrology, Vol. 1: The Ancient World", (first published as The Dawn of Astrology: a Cultural History of Western Astrology). London Continuum. ISBN 9781441181299.*

11. David Voas, (2007). *"Ten Million Marriages: A Test of Astrological 'Love Signs' "*. Carthie Marsh Centre for Census and Survey research, University of Manchester.

12. Dean Geoffrey, (2015). *"Love Signs Fail World's Largest Tests".* Available at http://www.astrology-and-science.com/S-love2.htm

13. Dean Geoffrey and Ivan .W. Kelly (2003). "Is Astrology Relevant to Consciousness and Psi?" *Journal of Consciousness Studies,* Vol. 10, pp. 6-7. Search at www.imprint.co.uk/jcs.html

14. Didier Castille, (2004). "Birth Day Effect on Natality Rhythms". *Correlation* 22.2, 20-32.

15. Divakar, Soundar. (2009). "The Science of Astrology". *The Astrological Magazine*, Vol. 98. Pp. 21-22.

16. Douglas W. Shrader (2007). "*Seven Characteristics of Mystical Experiences*". Presented at the 6th Annual Hawaii International Conference on Arts and Humanities, Honolulu, HI, (2008). Retrieved at http://citeseerx.ist.psu.edu/viewdoc/download ?doi=10.1.1.601.4094&rep=rep1&type=pdf

17. E. F. Weidner, "Historiches Material in der Babyonischen Omina-Literatur" *AltorientalischeStudien*, ed. Bruno Meissner, (Leipzig, 1928-9), v. 231 and 236

18. Frede, Dorothea, (2003). "Stoic Determinism," in B. Inwood (ed) *Cambridge Companion to the Stoics*. Cambridge: CUP, pp. 179-205.

19. Genovese, J.E.C. (2014). "A Failed Demonstration of Sun Sign Astrology",

Journal of Comprehensive Psychology Vol. 3 (16).

20. Gunter Sachs (1998). *"The Astrology File".* Published in paperback by Orion, London (1999).

21. Hamilton M.A. (2015). "Astrology as a Culturally Transmitted Heuristic Scheme for Understanding Seasonality Effects: a Response to Genovese (2014)", *Journal of Comprehensive Psychology* Vol. 4 (7).

22. Hand, Robert (1981). *"Horoscope Symbols"*, Whitford Press, Pennsylvania, USA.

23. Hartmanna .P., Reuterb .M., and Nyborga .H. (2005). "The Relationship between Date of Birth and Individual Differences in Personality and General Intelligence: A Large-scale Study". ©2005 Elsevier Ltd. Published online by *Personality and Individual Differences* 40 (2006) 1349–1362.

24. Hines T (1988). *Pseudoscience and the Paranormal: A Critical Examination of the*

Evidence. Buffalo, NY: Prometheus Books. ISBN 978-0-87975-419-8.

25. Holden, James Herschel (1996), *"A History of Horoscopic Astrology". AFA p. 1. ISBN 978-0-86690-463-6*

26. Houlding Deborah (2010), *"Essays on the history of western astrology",*'The medieval development of Hellenistic principles concerning aspectual applications and orbs'; *Nottingham: STA* Ch. 8, pp.12-13.

27. Hypatia's Astronomy http://lasp.colorado.edu/~bagenal/1010/SESSIONS/5.ScienceAstronomy.html . Retrieved 3rd April 2019.

28. "In This Issue". *Current Science,* Vol.96, No. 5, 2009, pp.624. Retrieved from http://www.jstor.org/stable/24104536.

29. Jeff Mayo; Christine Ramsdale (1979). *"Teach Yourself Astrology".* Ntc Publishing Group, p.5.

30. Jeffrey Bennett; Meghan Donohue; Nicholas Schneider; and Mark Voit (2007). *"The*

Cosmic Perspective", 4th Edition. Pearson/Addison-Wesley, Francisco CA, pp82-84.

31. Julie Beck (2018). "The New Age of Astrology", published in *The Atlantic*.

32. Kelly, Debra (2016). "10 Influential Astrologers that Shaped History." *List Verse*. https://listverse.com/2016/10/11/10-influential-astrologers-that-shaped-history/.

33. Manoj Kamoth (2009). "Testing Astrology", *Current Science*, Vol. 96, NO. 12, 25.

34. McGervey J.D. (1977). "A Statistical Test of Sun-Sign Astrology". *The Zetec,* Vol. 1, No. 2, p.53.

35. Michael Shermer (1997). *"Why people believe weird things: pseudoscience, superstition and other confusions of our time"* New York: W. H. Freeman and Company. ISBN0-7167-3090-1.

36. National Science Foundation (2014). National Center for Science and Engineering Statistics (NCSES) *"Science and Engineering*

Indicators 2014" Arlington, VA (NSB 14-
01), February 2014.
https://www.nsf.gov/statistics/seind14/index.c
fm/chapter-7/c7h.htm

37. Nick Kanas, (2007). *"Star Maps: History,
Artistry, and Cartography"*, Springer p.79

38. Nigel Henbest (1987), *"Misreading the Stars,"*
Word Press Review, September, p. 55.

39. P. A. H. Seymour, (1990). *"Astrology: The
Evidence of Science"* (Revised and extended
paperback version), Great Britain: Arkana-
Penguin.

40. Paul A. Heckert, (September 5, 2011). "The
History of Astronomy as an Example of
Scientific Methodology". *Decoded Science,*
Copyright © 2019 · Magazine Pro Theme on
Genesis Framework. Retrieved at
www.decodedscience.org/the-history-of-
astronomy-as-an-example-of-scientific-
methodology/2867   3rd April 2019, 6:05pm.

41. Paul R. Thagard, (1978) "Why Astrology Is A Pseudoscience". Philosophy of Science Association Journal, Vol. 1, pp. 223-234.

42. Paul Recer (1988). "Scientists Find Fault With Astrologers' Use of Stars," The Dallas Morning News, p. 6D.

43. Peters, Christian Heinrich Friedrich and Edward Ball Knobel (1915). *"Ptolemy's Catalogue of Stars: A Revision of the Almageist"*. Carnegie Institution of Washington.

44. Pankenier, David W., (2013). *"Astrology and Cosmology in Early China: Conforming Earth to Heaven", Cambridge University Press ISBN 9781107292246.*

45. Pingree, David, (1981) *"Jyotiḥśāstra, Wiesbaden: Otto Harrassowitz"* p.81.

46. Rudich, Vasily (2005). *"Political Dissidence Under Nero: The Price of Dissimulation".* Routledge, pp. 145–146. ISBN 9781134914517.

47. Saliba, George, (1994). *"A History of Arabic astronomy: planetary theories during the Golden Age of Islam"*. New York University Press. Pp.60-69. *ISBN 0-8147-7962-X.*

48. Saravana Kumar .G. (2014). *"Astrology— Heliocentric or Geocentric Model"*. Retrieved from https://innovativeastrosolutions.wordpress.com/20 14/04/26/astrology-heliocentric-or-geocentric-model/comment-page-1/

49. Sastry, T.S.K, K.V. Sarma, (ed.) *(1985)."Vedangajyotisa of Lagadha".* National Commission for the Compilation of History of Sciences in India by Indian National Science Academy.

50. Symons, S.L., Cockcroft, R., Bettencourt, J. and Koykka, C. (2013). *"Ancient Egyptian Astronomy"* [Online database]. Available at https://aea.physics.mcmaster.ca/index.php/en/ database/diagonal-star-tables

51. Teri Gee (2012). *"Strategies of Defending Astrology: A Continuing Tradition"*. Institute

for the History and Philosophy of Science and Technology, University of Toronto.

52. *The Humanist*, September/October, 1975.

53. *"The New Age of Astrology",* published in The Atlantic, (June 16 2018). Retrieved at: https://www.theatlantic.com/health/archive/2018/01/the-new-age-of-astrology/550034/

54. *"Theories of Astrology: A comprehensive survey"*. Retrieved from www.astrology-and-science.com/a-theo2.htm on 10th April 2019.

55. Titus Burckhardt (1977). *"Mystical Astrology According to Ibn 'Arabi "*. Beshara Publications, Abingdon, England.

56. Zarka, Philippe (2011). *"Astronomy and Astrology". Proceedings of the International Astronomical Union. 5 (S260): 420–425 (2011).*